50 THINGS TO DO with the REST OF YOUR LIFE

D1009092

Robert Pearce Wilkins

Library of Congress Control Number: 2003092032

ISBN 0-9608450-0-3

Published by:
R. P. W. Publishing Corp.
P.O. Box 729
Lexington, SC 29071

Printed in the United States of America

Acknowledgements

I want to thank my wife, Rose, for 47 wonderful years with more to come. Our lives would not have been as fulfilled without our children: Robby, Wally (gone but not forgotten), Sarah and Anne and their wonderful children; Gregory, Reese, Wallace, Baker, Wilkins, Anna and Robert. Several people also helped me over the years in my business life. Joy Fasenmyer, Jan Pollack, Dan Harmon and Aida Rogers—without them, many things in the book might not have happened to us.

I would also like to thank Martin and Wiggie Jones, Jimmy and Pat Brill, and Al and Betty Moses, who read the early draft of this book and gave me encouragement. And special thanks to Bob and Barbara Thomas and Elaine Gillespie (she designed the cover) for their many helpful suggestions. Special thanks to Rose. I think she has read the book at least 15 times.

Without Dan Harmon, this book would never have made it to you. Thanks, Dan.

I hope you will have as much fun reading the book as I did writing it.

Robert Pearce Wilkins

Contents

Introduction

I'm a lawyer by profession. My career has been dedicated to helping people plan their estates, whether modest or substantial. In this role I've observed intimately the unhappiness that befalls a few of my clients, both those of average means and those who appear to "have it all." A few of them—and I'm afraid this may apply to some of you—are letting their lives literally slip away. It isn't necessarily because they can't *afford* to do interesting things, but because they refuse to plan. They procrastinate. They simply never bother to factor the things they *really want to do* into their daily, monthly and yearly to-do lists. And in their minds, they have logical reasons why they can't do these things.

Away from my law practice, I've observed that some of my friends are in the same quagmire.

Forty years ago, I read a magazine article about a Boy Scout, perhaps 12 years old, who'd made a list of things he wanted to do with his life. A decade or so into adulthood, he looked back to review how many of them he had done. He was delighted to see he'd carried out many, many things on his list, largely because he'd *made the decision to do them* and followed through over a period of years. Of course, there were quite a number of things he hadn't done yet. He created a new list that was more in keeping with where he wanted to proceed at that stage of his life.

I then started making a list of things I wanted to do with the rest of my own life. Of course, I want to spend a lot of time enjoying my children and grandchildren—that's one of the most important things you *can* do. But there are an awful lot of other things you can do, too, if you make the time and take the time to do them.

As I went around the country speaking on estate planning and law practice management subjects, I would meet a lot of people, have dinner with them, do things with them. My favorite pastime was making them promise me they would go home and draw up a list of 10, 15 or 20 things they wanted to do with the rest of their lives. One of my greatest pleasures was seeing those people later and hearing them describe their lists and the things they'd done so far, and how this exercise really had made a difference in the way they lived. It can make a tremendous difference in your life, as well.

My wife Rose and I have been extremely active over the years. We have done many things with our kids and many things without them. Our lists of things we want to do periodically change—and that's natural. When you make your list, bear in mind that it isn't a list of things that have to be done tomorrow or next year. This list is "what I want to do with the *rest of my life*." Some of the things you list may be totally out of reach for now, but you hopefully will accomplish them in the future. As you grow older, new interests will replace a few of your earlier ambitions.

Put off the fun no longer. Start today. Start by . . . *making the list*!

—Robert Pearce Wilkins
Lexington, South Carolina
June 2003

1

Make the List

That's the obvious first step. Couples need to make separate lists. Then you need to get together and make a joint list, as well.

You won't really know what's going to be on your list until you sit down to compile it. If you're 30 years old, your list probably will be entirely different from the list of a 69-year-old. Over time, you'll be revising your list. For now, just *make that list—* and start doing at least one, two, or three of those things each year.

It's amazing: If you made a list when you were 30 and you did three of the things a year, then by the time you got to be my age, which is almost 70, you would have done 120 things you *passionately wanted to do*. In reality, Rose and I have done far more than 120 of the things we've listed over the years. If we hadn't focused on those, I'm convinced we would not have done nearly as much. It's so easy to do *nothing*—and then wonder what you did with your life.

We had our children make lists, and their lists were very different from ours. Robby, our oldest at 46, recently went to Costa Rica with his wife and two children for four months to simply enjoy themselves. Our daughter Anne and Robby's assistant Jan kept the real estate development business under control while he was away.

Obviously, your ability to achieve certain ambitions will depend on your pocketbook. But your list should include many kinds of things, some of which will cost little or absolutely nothing and some of which you can't afford now. Let me make a few suggestions to get you started.

Take a course in American history or any topic of interest. It may be a short course or audited course at a local college or technical school, or a tape or video or Internet program. Costs usually are reasonable; some educational opportunities are free.

Pushing that to the ultimate level, a list item for you might be to obtain a degree—a high school diploma, a college or technical college degree, an additional university degree, a master's or a doctorate.

Travel is high on our list. Where do you want to go? Some trips are expensive. Others cost almost nothing. Plan at least one or two trips each year.

Learn to paint, draw, take photos, cook, write poetry or speak a foreign language.

Give back to society by volunteering some of your time and talents.

Turn over to your children now some of the personal items you don't need anymore.

Make a journal of things you'd like to remember. I remember my wife-to-be Rose coming to Washington, DC, to work for Sen. Strom Thurmond while I was in the Army. I remember my first job on a tobacco farm, taking tobacco from the field to the barn behind a tractor—how sticky and gooey it was.

Learn to sail and race sailboats. That's one of the things my family did. As a result, we've gone as far as Montreal racing sailboats. My son Robby is still racing; he went to Sweden one year to compete in the J-24 world championships. My daughter Sarah sailed in the college finals in Washington state and she is the first woman Rear Commodore of our sailing club.

Ride a train. We went from Atlanta to New Orleans and back to attend the annual Jazz Festival. There were three couples; we booked a sleeping car (but just used it during the day as our private gathering place), and it was just a wonderful trip—not expensive.

Almost every sport has a place where you can go to learn how to play. Tennis is my sport. We have several facilities here in Lexington, SC, where we play tennis regularly. For you, it might be golf, softball or skiing.

Rose *loves* gardening. She became a certified Master Gardener, and her list includes different things she would like to do in that area of interest. She spends several hours a day either gardening or reading about it. She grows flowers, vegetables and fruits. When the seasons are right, we have wonderful tomatoes, lettuce, cucumbers, blueberries, blackberries and a variety of other things. There's nothing better than a fresh vegetable, and the best of the best are the ones you grow yourself.

Bird-watching is a wonderful thing to aspire to do. Serious bird-watching may be associated with photography. We have the largest purple martin roost in the country on the lake where we live.

I collect various things. Some collectors turn their interest and accumulated expertise into a business. Several of my friends go to flea markets, gather up certain types of items that interest them and then take them to a little antique mall to resell as specialty items. In this way, they make extra money to do other things they want to do with their lives, and they enjoy this endeavor as well.

Engage in some type of exercise program—essential for your health. Our wellness center in Lexington is inexpensive. Rose and I go and use treadmills and bicycles and weight machines. I found that the treadmill alone lowered my blood pressure 10 points.

For some people, starting a business is an achievable goal. It might be part-time or full-time. (I've tried so many businesses it's scary—the subject of another book I'm writing.)

The reason for making such a list and doing these things is to take charge of your life. Many people today have absolutely no control over their lives and make no attempt to take charge, and they're very unhappy about it. The simple act of thoughtfully preparing your list is your first step out of the bog.

After you make your list, you need to prioritize it. You may want to adopt or adapt some of the ideas that follow in this book—but not necessarily in the order in which they're presented here. Meanwhile, you may have designs of your own that we won't address. Determine which things are most important and most urgent to you, and which ones can wait.

Once you've prioritized your list . . . *begin putting it into action.*

2

Create a Schedule For Executing Your List

At one time, I committed to writing for one hour a day in my journal of recollections—one of the things on my to-do list. I very quickly realized I don't have that kind of discipline. I also tried devoting one hour a week to accomplishing one or another of the other things on my list.

Well, just stop and think about it. It's not that difficult to carry out, and it's a worthy aim. If you commit one hour, one day a week, that's 50 hours a year. You and I can do a lot in 50 hours.

So I decided to commit to three things a week, devoting one hour to each of them. I would write down the three things I wanted to do each week, and start doing them. If I could achieve those, I would be spending 150 hours a year on these *vital objectives* that were nearest to my heart.

Rose makes a daily to-do list. She says she would never get anything done without her list.

The point is that if you make a schedule for doing the things on your list, it's far more likely that you'll actually do them.

3

Make Audio & Video Recordings of You and Your Relatives

I started tape-recording and making home movies (now "videotapes") of my ancestors and relatives in the late 1960s. I have some wonderful videotapes and audio recordings of them telling their old stories, remembering their ancestors and what they did as children. It is really important to me.

If you haven't recorded your ancestors, consider doing it. There's a lot you and your descendants will want to know after your ancestors are gone, not only about them but about you when you were young. You can get it simply by sitting down with a tape recorder or video camera and listening to them reminisce.

I had an aunt and uncle who lived in Virginia. They had two children, and we visited them on occasion. On one trip during the '60s, I made a lengthy audiotape, primarily of my aunt. My uncle always said the thing that attracted him to her was her wonderful laugh. Naturally, when he said that, she laughed that laugh. On the audiotape, it's just priceless. A couple of years after her death, I copied the tape and gave it to her two children. I think they really appreciated that more than any gift I ever could have given them.

My mother's brother and sister in the 1910s used to ride horses from their homes to school—probably a mile or more. Uncle Frank used to love to tell the story of how, on a dare, he rode his horse up the steps and into the hallway of the school. The principal sent him home. He died recently, and I have that story on videotape in his own words—one of the favorite anecdotes of my family.

If you have old tapes of your relatives, you need to get the audiotapes transcribed. You need to consider getting videotapes transferred to more modern media.

Videotapes don't last long. Almost everybody is recording digitally now. I'm now looking at a DVD recorder which will allow me to record VHS and similar old tapes onto DVD or CD disks. My understanding is that this medium will last a very long time. I plan to make copies of those and give them to my children.

At the very least, you need to make copies of whatever medium you have and give them to somebody else. I always worry about the house burning down. I've gathered an incalculable store of information about my ancestors and about our children and about our lives. If my children have copies of these audio and videotapes, and something happens to any one of us, there'll be copies in other places.

I haven't taken the time to edit videos of my family, because quite frankly, I don't know that there's anything I'd want to cut out. I'd rather have the original recording than some Hollywood-esque production.

Rose and I have had very eventful lives. We've begun to record a little bit about ourselves, because there are a lot of things our children don't know. Maybe they won't care—but we care. Sometimes when we're on a trip, maybe back and forth between the beach and Lexington, we'll select a particular four- or five-year period and record what went on during that time. I get my assistant later on to transcribe that. We're working on our own little family history—not for publication but just for our own edification and for the benefit of our children and grandchildren.

You have to decide what makes the most sense from your perspective, but making audio and video records is extremely important. Aging parents and grandparents have much to tell. If you don't gather it while they're alive, it will be far more difficult for you to figure out later the things that happened and the kinships and geographic locations involving your ancestors. Don't forget that these parents and grandparents know things about their (and your) ancestors that you might never know. Get them on tape!!!!!

4

Give Something Back

Whatever your career, it's important to become involved in the organization or organizations that represent your field. In my case, those were the South Carolina Bar and the American Bar Association (ABA). I became active in them when I started practicing law. This not only benefited my practice, but it also led me into some fascinating things and off to some wonderful places I'd never imagined. The friendships and associations I forged over the years are truly part of the spice of life.

I have a lawyer friend who was not involved at all in the ABA until well into his career. He handled domestic relations law. I encouraged him to join the Family Law Section of the ABA. He became very interested and involved and ultimately became the section chair. Recently, he received an award from the ABA for his service.

In my own situation, I was involved in the Real Property, Probate and Trust Law section of the ABA. At that time, there was no specific ABA section for what became my professional "pet project": improving the *economics* of law practice.

Some of my new lawyer friends from around the country started a new Legal Economics Section (now the Law Practice Management Section) of the American Bar Association in 1974. Our objective was to show lawyers how to manage their practices more efficiently and represent their clients more effectively. I was fortunate to be the first editor of its magazine *Legal Economics* (now *Law Practice Management*). After six years I was honored to be the chair of this section. Later, I started a magazine for the Real Property, Probate and Trust Law Section of the ABA called *Probate & Property* and served as its founding editor. About two or three years later, I started *South Carolina Lawyer*, the magazine for the South Carolina Bar, and served as its founding editor.

These projects, as you might imagine, were extraordinarily time-consuming. During a 10- or 15-year period in the 1970s and 1980s, I probably provided a thousand unpaid hours a year to my state and national bar associations. On the other hand, the rewards were inestimable. Some of my dearest friends today are individuals in different parts of the state and nation whom I got to know while performing this volunteer work. These activities allowed me to travel with many of them all over the United States and to Canada, England, Scotland, Germany and Australia for meetings and activities.

The two service areas I enjoyed most outside my career were appointive jobs. I was asked to serve on our district public school board, and kept that post for eight or nine years. That was a highly satisfying experience for me. Today, I'm a member (and have served as chairman) of the Riverbanks Zoo Commission in Columbia—one of the most personally satisfying services I've ever performed.

Rose, meanwhile, has become a Master Gardener and is very involved in local and national beautification projects. She also became a Master Waste Educator and has taught and spoken on recycling and related subjects to a variety of audiences. She's contributed to the church and a number of other activities. Not long ago, she received an award from the Girls Scouts for being an inspiration to young girls.

She also worked as a poll manager in our county for some 20 years. Rose never was interested in running for public office, but she no less served our nation by participating actively in the democratic process.

Meanwhile, I served as president of our county's Republican Party convention for many years. In the distant past (1962), I even ran with others for the South Carolina House of Representatives (the first full slate of Republicans since Reconstruction—we were soundly trounced). Regardless of whether you're a Republican or Democrat, if you like politics, there are lots of ways to get involved. If you're not a political candidate, you still can take part, from the local precinct level to the national level.

You can contribute with monetary or material donations (valuables that can be either used or auctioned by your beneficiary organization). Alternatively, you can contribute your time as a volunteer. Many retired educators now offer their invaluable knowledge and time in a wide array of instructional programs. People of all ages work at Habitat for Humanity building sites, or help staff food and clothing banks in their communities. Join a litter clean-up campaign—or organize one—for your neighborhood or for a particular stretch of highway near you.

Typically, you won't receive public recognition for these kinds of endeavors. The personal satisfaction, however, is worth more than all the accolades in the world. I truly believe you ought to give something back to the profession that provides you with your living, and to society in general.

5

Organize Your Stuff & Get Rid of the Junk

What good is having it, if you can't find it? I have more stuff in my home office than you can imagine. It's in boxes, old files, on the floor, in the shelves and on the computer. Usually, but not always, I can find the stuff in the computer. I finally said that I was sick of the stuff on the floor, in the boxes and on the bed in the next room. It was either going to be organized or thrown in the trash.

I can't do it all in a day. It probably will take months because a lot of it came from my ancestors and I have to go through it carefully to make sure I don't throw away something that would make me cry.

I have always kept photographs and other memorabilia in big notebooks which are generally identified by year. Some are identified by the name of an ancestor. I decided to continue to put all items of this sort in these notebooks. But I want new notebooks for other categories—off the floor and into notebooks. At least I then can find what I am looking for.

I have a substantial number of computer programs, owner's manuals and other items associated with hardware and cameras I have purchased—they are everywhere and I can never find what I need. I went to a dollar store and bought four small plastic cabinets with three drawers each. Now all those items are in separate drawers and labeled so when I need them, I can find them.

Also, I bought two boxes of 100 file folders. I began putting things I wanted to keep in labeled, alphabetized file folders and then put them in boxes (labeled by category) or file cabinets in my home office—the only office I have. Will I be able to find this stuff? I hope so. At least it's organized.

What's left over won't fit in a file folder, so I need another kind of storage for those items I want to keep. I am using plastic boxes that I can label. (I also bought them from the dollar store.) So whatever is left over is likely junk.

Obviously, you have to use your own technique.

Let me suggest that you get rid of the junk. The reason is twofold: 1) to simplify your life and 2) to ensure that your heirs know, by what's left, those things which are really meaningful to you.

We all have junk of one type or another. The saying that "one person's junk is another's treasure" is certainly true. You and only you know what constitutes junk in your own life. But if you look around your house, you probably can identify at least some of the things that are undeniable junk.

Some things were junk the moment you acquired them, but you may have had an ulterior reason for the acquisition (they were a gift you couldn't refuse, they were a purchase you made in support of some cause, or they were on sale and you just couldn't resist the idea of the "bargain"). Certain other things were of real use or significance to you at some point previously, but they no longer have any importance at all. They're simply occupying space.

If you can't sell them or give them away, throw them away— but be careful about what you think certain items are worth. Go to several antique malls or consignment stores and ask. You may be shocked by what your mother's old waffle iron will bring.

Some of the things you don't want any longer may be classified as "junk" in your mind but may be worth something to homeless or less fortunate people. See the next chapter on making gifts to charity.

6

Donate Unneeded Items to Charities

It recently occurred to me that in my closet were some suits I hadn't worn in five years. Other clothes literally were buried in there. I wasn't sure exactly what was there. So I spent a day going through it. I picked out most of the things I had not worn in the past few years. Rose has done the same thing in her wardrobe. We have donated those clothes to a widely respected Columbia charity organization called the Oliver Gospel Mission, or to the Salvation Army or some other clothing charity.

You'll be amazed at how much junk is in your closet that you no longer need. The same goes for your basement or your attic or your garage. There almost certainly are items there that you no longer need, but that might be a boon to someone else. You may have furniture that is of no sentimental value to you or your children. There may be other things that just seem to have found a home in your storage rooms. These are items other people could use—and need. If you personally know individuals who might have a use for them, offer the goods to them first. Otherwise, donate them to charities.

As a practical matter, you almost always can obtain tax deductions for donated items if you itemize your deductions. Most charities provide you with receipts for donated items.

Over the decades, I've collected a large library of African-American music. Most of these blues and R&B recordings are old 78-, 45- and 33⅓-rpm disks that most people today no longer have the hardware to play. The Music Department of my alma mater, the University of South Carolina, has established a new African-American music center, so I contacted the staff and asked if they would be interested in these vintage records. They were indeed! After they examined my collection, we came to a win-win agreement: I would donate the disks to the center, and in return they would transfer selected recordings to modern CD media and give me a copy of the set, so I can continue to enjoy the music for many years.

It goes without saying you will likely get a charitable deduction for these gifts. (See Chapter 21.)

7

Write a Journal Of Things You Remember & Cherish

I haven't done this to the extent I want—but I'm determined to make myself do it at least weekly.

Make yourself a schedule for compiling your journal. Say, "I'm going to write down or record once a week [not once a day—once a day will wear you out] things that were especially important to me in my life, things I'd like to remember and things I think my children might like to read about after I'm gone—perhaps even before I go."

Here's an example that's going into my own journal:

As a child, only 10 or 12 years old, one of my first jobs was driving a tractor pulling drags from a tobacco field, where workers with mules pulling the drags had been cropping the tobacco—pulling it off the stalk. (Let me observe, as an aside, that when you touch green tobacco leaves during harvesting, it leaves a sticky black residue on your hands. After working with tobacco all day long, you have a major league wash job before you can come in for supper.)

In the barn, workers tied tobacco leaves to a stick, about three or four feet long—about the length of a broom stick—with a piece of string. Later, the stick with all the tobacco tied to it would be hung in the tobacco barn and the barn would be "fired" (I'll explain that momentarily) and cured. After it was cured, all the stickiness had gone away.

There were two kinds of workers under the shed outside the barn. "Handers" were the people who gathered together three or four leaves at a time and handed them to the stringers. Stringers had the responsibility for the stick. There would be a hander on each side of the stringer, handing the small bunch of leaves. Handers, who were usually women or younger children, made about $1.50 a day. The stringers, who were frequently women, made about $2 a day. The croppers in the field, who were mostly men, made about $4 a day. I made $1.50. Remember, this was in the 1940s.

After the leaves were strung on the sticks, the sticks were laid into a nice, neat pile. When the men would come in from the field at lunch and again at the end of the day, they would hang them up in the barn, starting at the top and working their way down. After the barn was full, they would "fire it up."

When I first started doing this, we were still "firing" or heating the barns with wood fires. Somebody would stay up all night, tending the fire. One of my most cherished moments was when I got to stay up and watch the older workers keep the fire going. I didn't sleep much; I wanted to see everything they were doing.

Later, when I was 12 or 13, they started heating the tobacco barns with fuel oil. My uncle owned a Pure Oil distributorship in Florence, SC. One of my jobs at age 14 and older was driving a truck down country roads, going around to the tobacco barns and delivering fuel oil. The oil normally went into 55-gallon drums that were at the back or side of the barn; in some cases the farmers had larger tanks, 200 or 250 gallons. Every now and then, a barn would catch fire and burn up. Fortunately, that was not an everyday occurrence.

Is that recollection of interest to anybody today? I don't know. It's interesting to me; I hope it'll be interesting to my children. It was almost 60 years ago, so I guess that makes it part of "history." Later, farmers changed the method for curing tobacco. Today, of course, there is a move to stop growing tobacco altogether. Regardless, to me that was a fascinating aspect of growing up in a tobacco community. Someday in the future, when historians are chronicling this particular way of life as it occurred during the

1940s, they may produce film footage of exactly what I've described above, and you or your grandchildren may find it interesting from the historical perspective. My own grandchildren and great-grandchildren, meantime, might shrug and say, "Ho-hum. My grandfather did that kind of labor a long time ago. So what?" But on the other hand, they just might say, "Wow! My grandfather did that kind of work when he was exactly my age! Cool!"

It doesn't matter what town or region of the country you're from, or what kinds of things you did when you were young. Make a record of them. Those recollections can become the "primary source" materials historians of the future will draw from. Even if not, they likely will fascinate some of your offspring.

8

Identify & Date Your Photos

Rose and I have three children and seven grandchildren. I've taken hundreds of pictures of them. Already, as I go back through them, I'm not sure which grandchild it is in some of these modern photos. I don't know how old they are in those particular frames. So I plan to gather my children and grandchildren and identify every photograph and approximately when it was taken.

Many of the photo processors today automatically print the date code on the back of each image. That's immensely helpful. But it's up to you to identify who or what is in the picture.

Photographs also need to be organized. Most of mine are at least in a notebook with the date the picture was taken, but I have some that never got there. That's work waiting to be done. Think about it. If you have a collection of photographs that have not yet been dated and identified, make time to do it.

Some companies today offer plastic sleeves for double-sided storage and a special, non-acidic paste for mounting them on the sheets that slide into the sleeves.

You need to do the same for photos you took on memorable trips. Identify them, date them, and organize them so that when your children are looking at them later, they'll understand.

Rose and I have been on many trips and we have numerous notebooks of photos from these trips. Fortunately, for the last 15 or so years, I have kept a journal of the activities on these trips and they are in the notebooks. I suggest that you consider keeping that journal, too. Even now we cringe to think what our descendants are likely to do with them after we're gone.

9

Start Your Own Special Interest Group

Most people belong to some organization—a book club, a bridge or poker club, a supper club, a church or scholastic or civic group, a garden club. If there are no clubs or groups in your town that interest you, think about organizing one yourself. Get your friends involved. Take turns meeting at one another's house. Plan meaningful activities for the group to do.

At one point, I was cooking pasta and having a wonderful time. I had about 10 pasta cookbooks and would prepare different types of pasta dishes. Three or four couples were in our "dinner group." Everyone would gather in the kitchen while I was cooking, and it became sort of a family thing. They would chat and sample wine and enjoy the meal.

The other couples had their own specialties to serve when we visited their homes. Overall, it was an unforgettable small group who got together to share food.

Rose belongs to several different interest groups that she considers very important in her life. For example, she has a luncheon group who gather once a month, each bringing a different dish for the others to sample. Meanwhile, I belong to a "canasta club." We have a meal and play games of chance. The stakes are very small; our primary interest (aside from the food) is the camaraderie.

The potential subjects that are worth sharing are endless. Your group may want to learn more about a certain country, historical aspect or travel destination. You may want to learn a language.

We've found that eight is about the maximum number of participants in a special interest group of this nature, for practical purposes. Matching schedules will be difficult enough for just two or three couples.

10

Start Making Your Travel Plans

Before you can start making your travel plans for each year, you need to make some basic decisions:

1. How much money can you budget for travel?

Sometimes you may need to know where you want to go, for how long, and how much each trip is going to cost you before you can set your budget. For our purposes let's simply assume that you know you have X dollars to spend on travel. (Also, see Chapter 19 on budgeting.)

2. From a time standpoint, how many trips can you make each year?

This depends on what kind of trips you plan to take. I would always start with the most expensive one or the one which is going to take the longest. Try to fit it in your schedule first. Don't forget to think about what the weather will be like at that time of year in the place where you are going. Once you've put the "big trip" on the schedule and see what it did to the budget, think about day trips and short two- or three-day trips that don't cost much.

3. Where do you want to go, and with whom?

Day trips can be fun and educational, and cost almost nothing. I have some suggestions for you on day trips in the Appendix.

A variation is a two-day trip, spending the night somewhere at or near your destination. This extends your range and allows you to devote concentrated study and exploration to aspects of the destination that pique your interest.

For longer adventures, we'll describe in a later section some of the programs offered by Elderhostels (see Chapter 15).

Other suggestions might include: Resolve to visit every state in the U.S. during your lifetime. I haven't achieved my objective yet; I'm missing Nebraska and South Dakota. At one time, one of my desires was to obtain a speaking engagement in every state. I made only 37 (and several foreign countries) before I retired— but I haven't stopped public speaking altogether, so it remains a "live" list item. There is a special section in the Appendix on my favorite destinations.

One of our children wanted to go to every national park. He hasn't accomplished that, but he's been to a lot of them. That's an excellent aspiration for individuals and families in almost every income bracket. Cabins and lodges at state and national parks cost relatively little. Unforgettable motoring vacations into Canada and Mexico likewise are within the means of most American families, with proper planning.

Turning your sights overseas, the first thing you should do is list the countries you eventually would like to visit. When you begin researching travel options in those countries, you may be surprised how little the trip can cost. With low airfares in the off-season, you can get there for next to nothing. You almost always can find nice hotels with modest rates. We found a hotel ideally situated in Paris for about $80 a night. The *concierge* was extremely helpful in suggesting restaurants and things to do.

The Number One trip of all time for Rose and me was a trip aboard the barge *Athos* in the southern part of France on the Canal du Midi. We put together a group that included three couples and a single, and we chartered an 80-foot tour barge. We each had a private bedroom and private bath. We had a crew of four: a captain, a cook, a cleaning staffer and a host/guide. The barge would go only a few miles a day; the total trip was 45 miles. You could walk alongside the barge or ride a bicycle (they furnished the bikes). We went through I don't know how many locks. Our barge host took us on tours of the towns and special attractions where we stopped. *Absolutely fantastic meals!* We were introduced to wines and cheeses from the region each day at lunch and dinner. We're primarily wine drinkers, but they offered other drinks, as well. The food was absolutely outstanding. To us, it was the most idyllic trip of all time.

We later took another barge trip aboard the *Liberté* in the Burgundy region of France, which turned out to be in our top five. It was very similar to the previous trip and was just a wonderful time, very laid-back. The food was great. The locales we stopped at were unusual, special kinds of places. For example, we visited a chateau where an artist was painting racecars on canvas for special exhibitions. In the garage of the chateau were vintage cars, several of which were valued at six figures.

French Country Waterways, Ltd. ((800) 222-1236) is the company we used for the *Liberté* trip. Several other companies specialize in European barges. You'll find plenty of options. We thoroughly enjoyed our excursions, and everybody who accompanied us felt the same way about it. It was reasonably priced, considering what we got. I would use a company that specializes in barges because they know which barges are best for your group.

We've been to New England three times, with different couples. The people who go with you can make or break the trip. We have five or so traveling couples and a single or two. We sometimes go alone. To me, it's a lot of fun to go with one or two other couples. Fortunately, all of our traveling companions meet this standard. If you're going in a car, it's pretty tough to deal with more than five people unless you get a big van.

On a barge or a ship, you can have a good time with as many as four couples. You can book the whole barge trip by yourself. On the other hand, if you book yourself on a barge trip with unknown others, you run the risk of having companions in relatively tight quarters who might be great or not so great. For our trips, we decided we'd rather put together our own group.

If you're going to take a trip with friends, don't go with too many. Eight is the maximum. Six is better; four might be the best of all. If you book a continental barge trip like those described in this chapter and you want to hold the cost within reasonable limits, it may take four couples to make that happen. But bear in mind that you're going to be in fairly close quarters on any trip.

Are Your Traveling Companions Compatible?

You have to make up your mind ahead of time—and this is absolutely critical to enjoying your experience—that everyone in the group is free to do whatever they want to do. Do not try to make everyone do the same thing at every stop. If most of you decide you want to go to a certain restaurant for dinner or to a particular tourist site, but several of your party don't really want to go, let them do what they want to do. In my opinion, this is the first rule when traveling with other people. Vocalize it.

In close quarters, you have to be able to get along extremely well with the people you're with. You have to measure their personalities against yours and everyone else's to make sure that's going to happen. Decide which of your friends you can travel with and which ones you can't. I'm sure a few of your friends are people you love dearly, but you would be absolutely miserable if you went on a trip with them. Good *traveling* companions are special friends. They're hard to come by. Enjoy them if you have an opportunity.

4. How much will each trip cost?

Decide what type of lodging you'll need. If I'm visiting a big city, all I'm going to use the hotel for is a place to sleep, so I'm not going to spend a lot of money on it. I've found many nice hotels/motels that frequently are very reasonably priced. We especially like hotels/motels that have suites with two bedrooms, two baths and a living room/kitchen in between. Amazingly, they frequently cost no more (or just a little more) than two double rooms. Why would I spend $200-300 a night for a room when I can find a nice room for $50-100 and spend the rest of the money on various things I want to do?

On the other hand, if I'm on an extended visit to a place like New England, I may use a country inn as my base for various excursions. Between excursions, I might appreciate the inn or a bed and breakfast that has a restaurant and comfortable nooks and common areas for lounging and reading and chatting with other guests. Consequently, I'll be much more willing to pay extra for lodging on that type of trip.

When we were in Paris, we stayed at the Grand Hotel des Balcons near the Luxembourg Gardens. It costs about $80 a night and is as nice a little hotel as Rose and I could ever want.

I have the same philosophy in regard to dining. I go to restaurants to eat. I have no interest in restaurants that charge $250 for a meal, because I can't tell the difference between a $250 meal and a $50 meal. If I were a food or wine connoisseur, maybe I would have a different attitude about dining expenditures.

Obviously, if you go with a group, what you get will be in the package price. Frequently, the transportation is included. If it isn't or you want to try for a better deal, read on.

5. How do you get there?

First, decide the most practical way to travel in order for you to derive maximum enjoyment from your trip—by automobile, train, plane or otherwise. If your objective is to explore certain attractions of a distant city, you probably will want to fly to that city and then make your way around by cab or rented car. If you have more time and if there are places and things you want to see between your hometown and your destination city, a road trip might be in order. On our last trip to New England in the fall, we flew to Boston, rented a car and drove through New Hampshire, Vermont, Connecticut, Massachusetts and Rhode Island. We stayed at reasonably priced inns along the way, and we ate reasonably priced meals. Another spectacular road excursion was the Big Sur drive in California.

A little later in this book we'll discuss getting airfare through credit card miles. Go shopping for your airline fares. I sometimes use my travel agent and at other times I make my own reservations.

Don't overlook cruise ships. They include your room, meals, entertainment, activities and sometimes transportation. There are some real bargains if you have time flexibility and go shopping. I personally like sailing ships and small cruise lines (140 passengers). (See the special discussion of this subject in the Appendix.)

Get Paid to Travel

If you are an expert on a particular topic or have an unusual talent that would be entertaining or educational to others, consider using your expertise or skill to make presentations in different travel destinations that interest you.

There are all kinds of possibilities. People make baskets, give speeches, provide instruction, display art, perform music. Even if what you have to offer isn't of broad enough interest to allow you to earn a living with it, it may be your ticket for fascinating travel opportunities. If people at least pay you a small honorarium or cover your expenses for your efforts, it may prove far more than worthwhile.

Most of my professional travels around the country were for the purpose of making speeches about estate planning or law office computerization. My first legal speech out of state was in Bismarck, ND, where the temperature was minus-40—a new experience for a southern boy. Later, I made several trips to Europe to speak to international lawyer groups. In most cases, I was not paid to make those presentations, but my expenses were paid. I wanted to go to those places and meet those people. It was a tremendous experience, and I would recommend it highly.

The reason I love traveling by ship is that the ship is your hotel. Your hotel goes with you. I *hate* packing and unpacking. On a cruise, you unpack on arrival—and that's it. You don't worry about packing up until it's time to go home.

One of the most important lessons Rose and I have learned is how to pack light. We don't carry a lot of baggage. We take one roll-on bag and one carry-on bag, and that's it. A number of travel catalog companies offer clothing designed for light packing and other travel gear.

Once you've sailed some of these ships, you become a member of their "regular group." They notify you of special deals from time to time. You might be offered a significant reduction in price, or a "twofer"—two passengers for the price of one. If you have a flexible schedule and you're able to book within 60 days, you can call them and ask what deals they have for specific destinations. That's when "twofers" most frequently are available.

11

Use Your Credit Card For Travel Mileage

Although credit card points can be used for many things, consider making all your purchases on a credit card that provides air miles. We've used American Express for years, and I can't tell you how many frequent flyer trips we've taken as a result of miles accumulated with our card.

Rose and I learned, probably 20 years ago, that by using American Express at every opportunity, we could get free mileage—or "points," which we could use for anything we wanted to.

Mileage made the best sense to us, since we wanted to travel. American Express miles can be used on most airlines.

We began to charge almost everything we bought on the credit card. I found that you can put some pretty high-ticket items on a card. We also use a Visa or MasterCard because there are some places in Europe and in this country that don't accept American Express. Some cards only give you miles on a specific airline.

You will need to see what card works best for you. Make sure that you get one mile per one dollar spent.

So now we accumulate free miles on these cards. It's seldom that we spend any money of consequence that we don't put on one of these cards.

I got so enthralled with this idea of using a credit card to get miles that at first, I was charging *everything* to a credit card. Rose, who reconciles our credit cards and pays the bills, soon informed me I should pay in cash for things that cost from $1 to $10, because it was driving her crazy trying to keep up with it. That's become our rule of the house: If more than $10, pay for it with the credit card; if less than $10, pay for it in cash.

Don't Accumulate Credit Card Debt!

The downside to credit card charges is that if you don't pay them off monthly, the interest rate is usually greater than you would ever pay if you had any other kind of loan. Make *certain* you pay off the credit card debt every month.

An alternative, if you can't pay off the credit card, is to get a short-term loan from the bank, which in most instances will be cheaper than the credit card interest rate. Make the interest rate comparisons.

12

Write Your Own Family Cookbook

Compile a cookbook of your mother's, grandmothers' or other relatives' favorite recipes and give it to members of your family. I have some recipes from my grandmother Pearce, who was born in 1869. I also have recipes from my mother, who was born in 1900, and my aunt, who was born in 1905. Some of these recipes are in their handwriting; others have had to be reconstructed.

My wife Rose is a very good cook and has her own special dishes. Her mother, born in 1908, has recipes—one being chili—that are now family classics. Rose recently compiled these recipes into *Treasured Family Recipes—From Our House to Yours*. In this cookbook, Rose lists the recipe detail and then adds a "Family Note" to tell whose recipe it was and its memories.

A keepsake of this nature would make an excellent Christmas present. The cookbook could consist of 20–50 recipes—more, if you decide to add specialties of other cooks. We included some of our children's favorites. Rose also included a few from other relatives and friends, which were served frequently at our house.

In today's computer world, it isn't difficult to assemble a book onscreen and print out as many copies as you want. We took ours to a local copy shop and they printed the pages on both sides and allowed us to either bind them with coils or put them in a notebook. You could add some appropriate pictures on the cover. If you produce a large recipe collection, you might want to pay a print shop to bind it more formally. We don't plan to sell ours. We make only enough copies to give to those friends and relatives who would really appreciate them.

If you don't do it, those recipes and those joyous memories will be lost. In most families, including ours, many of the best memories are those involving a meal.

13

Keep a Portable Note System

Get a small memo pad or calendar and carry it with you to record reminders and notable things that occur to you as you go through your day. If you have one of the new PDAs (portable digital assistants), use it. I like the old-fashioned way.

If I had to select the single greatest annoyance of my everyday life, it would be the little pieces of paper on which I write things I want to remember—and then I can't find the little pieces of paper. What I'm trying to do now is eliminate the small, easy-to-misplace slips of paper and write those items in a compact memo book, approximately 3x5 inches. I'm getting into the habit of writing most of the things I care about in my memo book. Of course, it won't work if I don't spend the few moments it takes to write things down.

I still have probably 150 tidbits of paper strewn everywhere, accumulated over a period of weeks and months. I need to go through them and preserve those notes I want to keep and throw away the rest.

One of the most useful pieces of software I have on my computer is a Day-Timer Organizer that allows me to keep up with addresses, phone numbers and the like. I use a paper Day-Timer to keep up with the tasks I perform during each day, but I use the software version to keep names, addresses, phone/fax numbers, e-mail addresses and Internet Web sites.

As I grow older, I find it harder to remember things. The little memo pad helps me with a lot of that, but it isn't a complete solution. For example, occasionally I'll start upstairs to do something, and my mind is racing to any number of things so that by the time I arrive, I've forgotten why I've trotted upstairs. (Don't laugh. If that's never happened to you . . . just be patient.) So I'll call

Rose on the intercom and ask her why I went upstairs. Equally bad: I'm driving and as I approach an intersection, I've momentarily forgotten where I'm headed and whether I'm supposed to turn right or left or go straight. I have to slow down and think about why I've come to that intersection. (Let me reiterate: If this seems weird to you younger readers, trust me—your time's coming.) I have friends who tell me they have the same problem.

The memo pad won't solve that dilemma, but it certainly can help solve the problem of capturing information you want to keep for later use.

14

Read Books

I like to read. My wife likes to read. Rose is the books columnist for *Sandlapper, The Magazine of South Carolina*, which we publish through a nonprofit company. We enjoy both fiction and nonfiction.

The fiction works I like the most are series which have continuing characters who appear in each book. The character is introduced in Book One, and by Book Fifteen the character still may be involved—or that character may have died off, but other recurring characters have been developed. There's nothing more exciting for an avid reader than discovering a new series that you like and that already has 12 or 15 titles in print, waiting for you to indulge, with more in the offing.

You may find a series of books that especially appeal to you. In almost every case, the various series I've started have been recommended to me by friends. In turn, I'll recommend three series here (if you've read my own book this far, I certainly consider you *my* friend ☺). Altogether, they represent 30–40 books.

W.E.B. Griffin is my favorite author. His books include "The Brotherhood of War" series about the Army and "The Corps" series about the Marine Corps (eight or nine books in each series).

Griffin's a wonderful writer. Probably the best I've read is the first in his "Brotherhood of War" series, *The Lieutenants*. All these books are in a wartime or service-related setting, but they're mainly about *people*. Rose normally doesn't like books about war and fighting, but after I persuaded her to read *The Lieutenants*, she became hooked, too. We both have read every book in the series and look forward to each new publication. We've introduced a lot of our friends to Griffin's books, and they've liked them, as well.

Another author I like a lot is Bernard Cornwell. His "Sharp" series is set in the Napoleonic era. Again, it's about war but it's also about people. It's very gory, so I didn't think Rose would like it. Surprisingly, she did like it and she's read all the volumes in the series (more than 10).

I like police stories and mysteries. The *Spencer* series by Robert Parker is one of my favorites. As you probably know, they made a TV series out of part of it. It's very well-written and easy to read.

Some readers don't care so much about a series as they do about its author. Dick Francis, for example, writes mostly about horse racing in England and is quite popular, but his books are not in series. The characters are different from one novel to the next.

I've read so many books that I have to keep a list so I don't buy books I've already read. I especially like mystery and lawyer stories. I've found that the best way for me to decide what I'm going to read next is to talk to some of my reader friends. We compare notes. I share my list with them and ask for their recommendations.

Consider maintaining your own "reading list." If you read a lot of books, it's helpful in keeping track of the ones you've read. It also is something you can share with others.

My wife and I both read nonfiction, as well. The nonfiction you select naturally is determined by your particular interests in life. We go to the library periodically and browse through those sections which appeal to us.

A new twist to the traditional "library lending" concept is the books-on-tape feature of the Cracker Barrel family restaurant chain. If you've dined at a Cracker Barrel, you know that each restaurant in the chain has a "store" side where you can buy a variety of folksy, old-fashioned items ranging from candies to early American-style toys. They also sell a notable selection of audiotapes and CDs. These include collections of period radio shows, and both classic and contemporary books on tape. What you may not realize about Cracker Barrel is that now, you can *rent* their books on tape. Rose and I, for a couple of our longer car trips, have gone to Cracker Barrel before leaving and rented a book on tape. We

---

Good Books Are Like Good Friends

Some of my other favorite authors are William Bernhardt, Jay Brandon, William Caunitz, Tom Clancy, Mary Higgins Clark, William J. Coughlin, Stephen Coontz, Michael Crichton, Frederick Forsyth, C.S. Forrester, John Grisham, Jack Higgins, John Katzenbach, Elmore Leonard, Gregory McDonald, Steve Martini, Christopher Newman, Patrick O'Brien, Richard North Patterson, Barbara Parker, Lisa Scottoline, Robert Tannenbaum, Joseph Wambaugh and Shelby Yastrow. I had to stop. I have more than 100 on my list of favorites. I'm sure you have your own favorites. I'm always open to book recommendations; please feel free to send along yours.

Amazon.com now sells used books as well as new ones. My wife asks me why I don't get rid of some of the ones I have. I probably have four or five hundred paperbacks, and I really do need to do something with them because they're causing a clutter. On the other hand, I like to keep them and lend them to friends who, in turn, share books with me. I've thought about giving them to a nursing home or prison but haven't taken the big step yet. Perhaps that's the unresolvable "collector's dilemma". . . .

listen to it during the drive and turn it in at another Cracker Barrel at the other end of the trip. You get some of your money back.

Rose and I have slightly different tastes in reading, but by and large we like the same things. If you and your spouse have common reading interests, it's a tremendous benefit both for your relationship and for your reading enjoyment.

15

Take Continuing Education Courses

Your local college, university or technical school probably offers diverse courses you never imagined were available. I've taken a couple of computer courses and a drawing course at our nearest technical school. The University of South Carolina, which is only a 20-minute drive from my home, allows citizens 65 and older to audit classes free, provided there's enough room in the class. I'm sure other universities do the same thing.

We had an 81-year-old friend who took a wide variety of courses over a 20-year period. He probably had completed enough course work to qualify for several degrees. Some colleges also allow auditing by younger students, under certain circumstances.

For those who don't have those opportunities close at hand, mail-order and Internet courses are available to fit almost any budget. In some situations, you can get small groups together and share the cost of the courses and/or supplemental materials.

I would suggest looking into The Teaching Company (**www.teach12.com**). It sells perhaps 100–200 CDs, videos and audiotapes of college professors teaching just about every subject known. Their instruction is outstanding. The regular prices may be too expensive, depending on your budget, but remarkable academic bargains are available for courses they periodically offer on sale. Check their Web site. Get on their list for special sales.

The first one I bought was "The American Civil War" by Gary W. Gallagher of the University of Virginia. I never had studied the Civil War thoroughly, and I decided I wanted to become more informed about it. Gallagher is a wonderful and, in my opinion, balanced teacher on the subject. It's a course of 48 lectures of 30 minutes each. I had it on audio CDs, which I kept in my car. When I was driving alone, I would listen to the CDs. (As a bonus benefit, incidentally, this prompted me to learn more about my car's CD player. When I stopped the car and returned later, I wanted my CD to begin where it had left off. After some experimentation, I found it was pretty simple: Leave the player on, cut off the car and when you get back in, cut on the car and there it is.)

I loaned that CD to a friend who teaches an Elderhostel course on the Civil War, and he thoroughly enjoyed it. In return, he lent me his CDs on "How to Listen to and Understand Opera" by Prof. Robert Greenberg of the San Francisco Conservatory of Music, and I had a wonderful time listening to them.

I'm presently about halfway through videos on Impressionist painters. Meanwhile, I'm listening to "The History of the United States," which is on audiocassette only. I went to Radio Shack and bought a portable audio player with earphones. When I go to the wellness center, I take along that course. Each class on tape lasts about 45 minutes. That keeps my mind occupied during my 30 minutes on the treadmill and 15 minutes pulling various weight devices, and makes the exercise experience much more pleasant.

Rose and I recently took a four-hour course at Johnson & Wales in Charleston, SC, on how to make stocks and soups. It was very, very interesting.

If you're 50 and older, you're eligible to enroll in Elderhostel courses. Rose and I have enrolled in only one Elderhostel course (painting with watercolor), but we're looking at a number of others. Elderhostel offers classes and outings in almost any topic that interests you. You can learn to play golf or tennis. You can birdwatch. Your can learn about history or art. Elderhostel has learning venues all across North America and in dozens of foreign countries. Some of the courses are designed specifically for grandparents to attend with their grandchildren.

Elderhostel prices are very reasonable. A week's session—which includes food, lodging and any required teaching materials—will be $350–500 per person. We've found probably 300–500 courses being held within 300–500 miles of where we live. What makes Elderhostel programs ideal is that they're inexpensive, and many of them are within driving distance of your home.

Some of the accommodations are more rustic than others and require a bit of adjusting. We shared a bath, for example, when we enrolled for the watercolor course at the John C. Campbell Folk School in the North Carolina mountains (we prefer a private bath). Other courses involve lodging in a motel. Some of the accommodations are extremely nice. You can determine the general lodging arrangements from the course descriptions.

Regardless of the arrangements, you're almost certain to have a good time and learn something worthwhile. You'll also meet some interesting people. Elderhostel, Inc. is located at 11 Avenue de LaFayette, Boston MA 02111-1746; **www.elderhostel.org**.

Self-Instruction

In many areas, you can further you education on your own. You simply need to make time and apply yourself.

Over the years, my wife Rose has become a magnificent cook—and now she's determined to make me a cook. (I am trying hard.) As I discuss elsewhere in this book, she also took it upon herself to become a Master Gardener. She completed the required program instruction, but much, if not most, of her knowledge about gardening she acquired on her own. She committed thousands of hours to reading, exploring gardens, scrutinizing plants and soils, amassing tips from other gardeners, and a lot of trial and error.

Improving my bridge skills was one of my own goals. I found a computer program called Bridge Barron 11 that allows me to develop my skills by playing against the computer. I have friends who have advanced their caliber of chess play in the same way.

16

If You Are Religious, Get Involved

If religion is important to you, broaden your involvement—and stay involved. Rose and I were among the founding members of our local Episcopal Church. Rose has served as junior and senior warden and as a member of the vestry for many years.

Religion means a lot to many people. Take part in the different programs your religion sponsors. If you have leadership skills in certain areas, offer to serve as a leader.

17

Make Time for Important Things

Strike "I don't have time" from your vocabulary. Do what makes you happy. You can find the time.

It makes me ill when friends tell me they don't have the time to do some of the things that interest them. It's because they don't put any order into their lives. They don't establish priorities.

It's amazing what happens. If, for example, they get sick, everything seems to work out okay; they simply return to their work and their other obligations and activities after they get well. If a close friend or relative is in need, they find the time to visit and help that person. But when it comes to what they want to do themselves, they don't have their lives prioritized.

It makes some people feel important to have more to do than they can do. But one result is that they usually fail to do those things which really make them happy.

How do you accomplish the things you want to accomplish? Get up earlier in the morning, if you have to. Set a specific time period for doing certain things. Determine, for example, that "on Wednesday at 5 o'clock, I'm going to do something that makes me happy—and nothing is going to get in the way." Plan everything else around that. Decide what you want to do with your weekend or your day off, and do it.

Prioritizing your life is the key. It's just too easy to say, "I can't do it because I have all these other things I have to do." In fact, you *don't* have to do most of those other things, or you can do them at a different time. The things you don't want to do, rather than the things you do want to do, should be the things you "don't have time for."

18

Keep Your Mind Sharp

I love crossword puzzles. I work the puzzle in our local newspaper every day. It's easy enough that I usually can complete it without much help. After about five years of struggling with a variety of challenging puzzles, I ultimately bought a crossword puzzle dictionary. I use it only when I'm totally stuck.

Can I solve *The New York Times* crossword puzzle? Absolutely not. It's no fun for me, because it's too hard. Can I do the *USA Today* puzzle on my own? Well, I can do Monday, Tuesday and Wednesday. I think they make them harder as the days go by; I have trouble with Thursday and Friday. (Incidentally, you can go online to *USA Today* and print out its crossword puzzles and solutions on your computer.)

My wife and I like to play bridge. As I indicated earlier, I enjoy a computer bridge game called Bridge Baron 11. With a game of this type, you can play bridge against the computer—and the computer is pretty smart. You bid and play the hand. At each step, the "Bridge Baron" will offer suggestions as to what, in its opinion, you should do. I prefer to make my own plays, although sometimes I might see what the Bridge Baron would do, just for fun. After you've played the hand, you can let the computer play the hand and then study how your play compares with that of the computer. The software's scoring technique lets you compete against the computer as you play.

There are many exercises and games you can use to keep your mind sharp. Notice I chose the verb "use" in the preceding sentence. When you reach retirement age, you no longer need to justify the time you spend playing. Fun things, in fact, become progressively more important to your health. Medical science makes it clear that individuals who keep their brains active are less prone to many of the disabilities commonly associated with "old age."

19

Make a Budget for Your 50 Things

Some of the things you'll want to do with the rest of your life will cost money. You have to examine what kind of finances you have.

It's relatively simple to prepare a budget. How much money comes in, and how much goes out? Now you know what's left. If you examine your last year's numbers, you'll have a pretty good estimate of what's in store this year. You can draw up your budget with a pencil and pad, or with a computer program such as Quicken or Microsoft Excel.

There are two ways to accommodate your "rest of my life" list in your budget. One is passive: "How much money do I have left over after other expenses to put into my travel fund or my favorite charity or my favorite activity?" The other is proactive: "I would like to spend X amount on travel and Y amount on charity and Z amount on my favorite indulgences. Now, where do I find this money? Is there anything in my existing budget that I can cut?"

Obviously, your income and available resources will determine what kind of budget you can have. I personally operate on the assumption that whatever I spend on travel or personal interests should come out of excess income. Generally, I should not be using my principal to fund these kinds of things. But if you have enough, you might.

Don't lose sight of the fact that a lot of fun and interesting things can be done at very modest cost, if you're vigilant for bargains and alternatives. Many things—learning photography, keeping a journal or playing tennis—are inexpensive or almost free, beyond an initial investment. Traveling and indulging yourself are usually the things that will require substantial expenditures.

20
Consolidate Your Debt

If interest rates are low or going down, it's a great time to consider consolidating your debt. You need to sort out the interest rates you're paying on your various loans and credit cards. You might ask your existing lender(s) for a rate reduction, or look into obtaining an equity line on your house.

21
Spend Your Own Tax Dollars

I'm annoyed with the United States government (not to mention state government). There are many things I like about it, but I hate the fact that it takes my money and wastes much of it. Obviously, the government must have money to operate, but far too much government spending goes to inefficient bureaucratic overhead and to pork barrel projects in which I have zero interest. If I sound like a congressional candidate, don't worry; I'm just a long-time frustrated taxpayer. You undoubtedly are, too. (I don't believe I've ever met an American taxpayer of any age, sex, race, creed or political inclination, from any part of the country, who is altogether *happy* with the percentage of her or his income that's claimed by taxes, or with the way the government is spending the money.)

There are legitimate ways to withhold some of your tax money from the government and spend it the way you want to. I don't know how much of your money you give to charity now, but keep in mind that charitable giving is tax-deductible, if you itemize your deductions.

I personally want some of my money to benefit churches; charities that aid the needy, such as the Salvation Army or, in our state capital, the Oliver Gospel Mission; the University of South Carolina (my alma mater) and its law school; the South Carolina Bar Foundation; and several other institutions. I'm sure you have your own preferred charities. Whatever they are, you need to understand the math.

To the extent that your charitable gift is deductible, it should reduce your taxes, dollar for dollar. You, of course, have given the specified amount to the charity, but since you get a deduction and thus it reduces your taxes, it means the government has made a contribution, as well.

There are some limitations on these deductions, and the law is changing constantly. Discuss the idea with your tax professional.

Whether you decide you want to do this, and to what extent, depends on three things: 1) how much money you have left over in your budget after your expenses, 2) what tax bracket you're in and 3) how strongly you believe you'd like to benefit charity rather than have the government waste your money.

Think about it. For some of you, making a charitable donation will be for the principle of the thing. For others, it will be a planned use of your money to benefit a certain charity you want to help (which may be one of the 50 things you have on your master to-do list)—with the government, in effect, making a substantial percentage of that contribution for you. You're saying, "Uncle Sam, I'm giving X dollars to the Harvest Hope Food Bank, and I'm sure the food bank appreciates very much the portion that you've decided to contribute." No legislative debate or delay or political bickering is required. You don't have to phone your senator's office. It's your money to begin with, and this is one bit of "government spending" you get to determine entirely on your own.

22

Get the Job That Makes You Happy

This is an interesting concept, because some people say, "Listen, I have to make a living." Well, you just might find you can make a living doing something you like.

In some cases, the need to support a family might result in a person struggling in a hated job while yearning for a different job. You have to determine at what point in your life you can do both things—support your family *and* get the job you really would like. Obviously, things change, depending on whom you've got to support. With four kids under age 6, which we had at one time, you may not have the flexibility you'll have later when the children are away and on their own.

I know people who have moved to South Carolina and started bed-and-breakfast inns, who had entirely different kinds of jobs elsewhere. How long they like running bed-and-breakfasts remains to be seen. But that's an example of people leaving ordinary jobs—in some instances jobs they did not like—and doing something different.

Bite the bullet. Make whatever sacrifices are necessary to obtain the kind of career you want. Far too many people go through life with jobs they don't like. In some cases, it may be the only job they can get, at least for the time being. But in other cases, it's really a question of deciding what they want to do with their lives. Determine the job that's going to make you happy, and go get it.

Much depends on your long-term objectives. For many people, a simple job with good benefits, basic hours and no headaches makes them happy because they have other passions they want to pursue. They can get a job they like (or at least easily tolerate). It might be a government job that has regular hours, gives you good time for vacation and other benefits, and allows you to do those other things with your life which you really want to do. You can spend more time with your children and engage in any number of fascinating pursuits. The job primarily provides your financial base, for current purposes and retire-

Again, It's a Budget Issue

Most people don't do a budget to determine how much money they need to live and do what they want to do. They may find that they really can live their dream, if they make an effort. Some people have been able, by budgeting, to break away from jobs in big cities and move to small towns to do things that make them extremely happy.

ment purposes. Obviously, any number of government jobs, either state or federal, fit this bill very nicely. Many private-sector jobs can accomplish the same objective.

Where Do You Want to Live?

One objective of a new job may be to allow you to move where you'd like to be geographically. You may like your present job, but you don't like where you're living.

As for me, I have no desire to live anywhere else. I've lived in South Carolina almost all my life. I love it here. However, I know a lot of people who have moved here from points north, for example, because they got tired of the cold.

Moving to another place may impact your career objective, or be impacted by it. I know many people who carefully considered those two factors together before making their great life change: job satisfaction and desired locale. While you're reevaluating your career, you should reevaluate your total situation.

You might be surprised to discover that some of your most interesting, multi-talented, widely traveled, extremely well-read acquaintances hold down jobs that strike you as anything *but* fascinating. It's likely these individuals have determined that their jobs are simply the means to enable them to be and do all those other things that impress you about them. They don't care to be known for what they do at work. They want to be known for the various other things that are made possible by their work. The jobs that make them happy are the ones which facilitate their "50 Things to Do With the Rest of My Life" lists.

Other people have a dream to make their mark in a particular profession. Sometimes that's very difficult to pursue. If you have a large family to support, for example, you might not be able to leave your unfulfilling but secure current employment and go for your dream—not right now, at any rate. On the other hand, you actually might be in a position to make that change but don't realize it. At least reexamine your alternatives and strive to make the Big Change by a certain point in the future. Don't fall into the rut of a glum daily routine that frustrates your spirit and makes you an unbearable grump to be around. Look at where you are now and where you would like to be.

23

Learn to Do Something You've Always Wanted to Do

Make the time—now—to learn how to do something new that makes you happy. We've already mentioned learning how to paint and play a sport. Those are only two examples out of *thousands* from which to choose. Open your imagination.

Maybe you've always wanted to master a few card tricks to entertain friends at parties and dinners; books on card tricks are available. Maybe you want to try your hand at soap sculpture; again, books are available—and soap bars aren't difficult to come by in this country. Maybe you have a fine singing voice which you've never exercised; consider joining a church choir or community choral society—or, if you can accompany yourself on guitar or piano, line up a "gig," just for fun, at a neighborhood restaurant. (Who knows *who* might be savoring lasagna and Chianti a couple of tables down the wall from your corner perch?)

It may be that you have several or many personal interests you want to explore. Painting may be something that intrigues you, but you don't feel you have the natural skill for it. You have to play with it and decide whether to commit more of yourself to painting, or turn to a different area of interest.

Photography can be an exceptionally rewarding hobby. Learn to take pictures. Courses probably are offered at a nearby technical school or university, or at a civic or community recreation center.

Do you dance? Do you *not* dance but wish you could? Then learn how. Learn from friends, or take a course.

As for me, I've pursued a number of different interests in my life and, frankly, weeded out a few that simply don't work for me. I've tried playing the piano and guitar, for example, and decided those aren't among my skills (I'm the ultimate monotone, when it comes to music). But the point is that I did attempt them, and now I don't have to wonder for the rest of my life whether I *might* have become a guitar impresario if I'd only given it a chance. I gave it a chance, and now I'm giving some other things a try, things that are of equal interest to me. I've discovered that I can do some of those things pretty well, actually, and they bring me priceless enjoyment.

Sports give you a wonderful opportunity to do things with other people. I played slow-pitch softball for 20 years and developed a great group of friends. It was a wonderful activity. After each softball game we would go to a local grill where they had good food.

Sailing was our most active sport when we were bringing up our children. Three of our children became very active in sailing. We would go to out-of-town regattas. Rose and our two girls, who at the time did not sail because they were too young, would get with the other children and play and have a wonderful time.

Our son Wally would sail with a good friend of ours, and I'd sail with our older son Robby, and we'd have a wonderful weekend. We did this as many as 10 or 15 times a year for about 10 years.

I've played tennis in all kinds of environments. I've played in volleyball tournaments all over the country. I've played a game called half rubber, similar to stick ball, which is unique to Charleston and Florence, SC, and Savannah, Georgia. They're all wonderful experiences. I've made many new friends.

Fishing. Golf. Hunting. Camping. Hiking. If any of these activities interest you, put them on your list. Some sports can be done with church groups, neighborhood groups, groups of company employees. Some can be done with children and grandchildren. Others have to be done individually or in a different environment.

In South Carolina, at least, quite a number of wellness recreation centers offer courses in all kinds of things. I took a course in yoga, which for me was sort of a joke. I was the only male in the class; all the women were able to do all the movements with their legs and arms; I had difficulty doing any of that. So about halfway through the course, I decided that was not for me. But not every course is one that you lose on.

But if you're not willing to go out and get involved, none of these things will happen. Simply *try* things you think you *might* like to do. See where they take you. Let them make you happy.

24

Indulge Yourself

Make a list of things in which you would like to indulge. I'm not sure at what point you should make this list—which is not to be confused with your master list of things you want to do with the rest of your life. This is a list of special things you might want: a car, a sailboat, a kayak, a gazebo, a swimming pool.

Sit down and make a list of five things with which you would like to indulge yourself. If you're married or have a a close friend, you need two lists and a joint list. Some of the items just aren't going to work within the context of your existing budget. Others may be cheaper than you thought.

Let's say one of the things you want is a swimming pool. Perhaps all your children are young, and by the time you're able to afford it, they'll all be out of college. Maybe what you should do is decide how high it is on your list. If it's high enough, you may be willing to go into debt for it and allocate X amount of dollars in your annual budget to retire that debt over a specified time period. If you do it well, the pool may enhance the value of your home for resale purposes, which makes it a truly justifiable investment. It certainly makes sense, if you can arrange for it, to have the pool while your children are at home and are of an age to enjoy it. If you keep your home, your grandchildren will begin to enjoy it, as well. Even if you never sell the home and in that way "recoup your indulgence/investment," it will pass on to your heirs, who are likely to continue enjoying the swimming pool for many years. Either way, you're likely to get your money's worth for that particular kind of indulgence.

I'm not saying you should do *whatever it takes* to buy a swimming pool. Depending on your circumstances, buying a pool may be a serious mistake. I'm simply pointing out that in some cases, you can amortize the cost of your indulgence over a period of time, if it won't fit into your present budget, and receive the benefits of it during the pay-off period. For "indulgence" items of this sort, you likely will need to set aside a special budget.

You have to remember, when compiling your list of indulgences as well as your overall "Things to Do With the Rest of My Life" list, that it's foolish to plan too many of those things for the distant future. You may not be here 5 or 10 years from now, or you may not be physically able to do certain things at that time.

In most cases, your indulgence items should be things you will enjoy over and over again, not just once.

25

Every Day, Tell Someone You Love Him/Her

It doesn't have to be the same person each day. It might be a child, might be your spouse or your close friend, might be a grandchild, might be your mother. Could be anybody.

Don't say it just to say it; say it because you mean it. A lot of people don't say it because they're embarrassed to say it. A lot of people don't say it because it never occurs to them to say it. I can assure you the person on the other side will always remember it. When you're gone, they'll always treasure the fact that you told them you loved them.

26

Do Something Nice For Someone Every Day

It doesn't have to be anything special. It could be simply a nice response to someone who's being ugly. I was at a football game recently at which our team lost. We were walking back to our cars and some folks from the winning team were berating us, until a gentleman in our group walked over to them and said, "I thought your team played a great game. I'm sorry we lost, but your team was just better than ours today." The silence that followed was absolutely amazing, as was the way the attitude of those people changed as they walked on down the street.

We *can* make a difference. Americans have become too busy, too unfriendly, too aggressive. A nice attitude and an unexpected polite word or kind act can not only embarrass a hostile person, but bring about a positive change. It can make an aggressor wonder, "Why did I do something that bad?" Hopefully, it will change that person's attitude.

You can do something as simple as holding the door open for someone who has an armful of packages. When you're driving in thick, crawling traffic and you come upon a signaling vehicle off to the side whose driver obviously has been waiting to get in line, make room. The time that additional car length will cost you at the end of the traffic jam will amount to two seconds or less.

If you converge with another shopper at a check-out counter, let the other person go first. And if the check-out clerk bungles your tab and has to call for the manager to come clear the register, don't fume and broadcast your annoyance as the line builds behind you. Smile and offer, "You must get tired, working on your feet all day."

Learn the "code language" of civility. For example, when I say to you, "Hello, I'm Bob Wilkins," one of the things I'm doing is asking *you* for *your* name.

It certainly will make you feel good about yourself when you do something nice for someone else, something you weren't expected to do. The look on the other person's face and the thank-you is more than worth it.

27

Avoid Fights

There are no winners in a fight, only varying degrees of losers. The line between fighting and arguing can be very thin. If you're married, you certainly realize no two people can live together without arguments. For many happily married couples, these occur daily. Learn how to resolve them in a way that does not leave either party with a feeling that the other person has taken advantage or done something wrong. Walk away from an argument once you've both said what you wanted to say; to pursue it any further is likely to create or escalate bad feelings.

My wife Rose has one of the best rules I've heard in this regard: Don't go to bed mad. Resolve your differences before you go to bed. If your disagreement does evolve into a fight, there's nothing wrong with saying, "I'm sorry." If you say you're sorry, the other person likely will apologize, too, and you can get on with your lives. The fight probably wasn't important anyway.

While we're on this subject. . . . Don't simply avoid fights—go out of your way to make friends, not enemies. You can't have too many friends on this planet. Make new ones, and cultivate the ones you already know.

28

Learn to Use the Internet

To me, it's mind-boggling to think of all the useful things you can find on the Internet. But they won't be useful to you if you can't find them.

I can't offer you even the most elementary introduction to using the Internet in these pages, but let me tell you about an excellent starting point to consider once you acquire the basics: Google.com. Google has become my favorite Internet "search engine." When you go to the **www.google.com** Web address, you find a simple search page with a blank field. Your cursor is blinking at the beginning of the blank box, waiting for you to type in a subject or name about which you want information. Then you press the <Enter> key, and Google performs an amazingly quick but fairly thorough search of the Internet for all the Web pages it indexes that contain your search term, either in the title of a page or in the body of the text on that page.

I recently went to Barbados to catch a Royal Clipper cruise ship. I wanted to find information about Sam Lord's Castle on Barbados, a place my AAA agent had recommended. I went to Google and typed "Sam Lord's Castle" (within quotation marks—which orders a specific search for those three words occurring together). The search almost immediately returned a full page of "hits" (Internet site listings), one of which was the facility's home page on the Internet. I obtained all the information I wanted, at a cost of very little time and no fee, from the convenience of my home computer keyboard.

Once you learn to use a search engine like Google, you can "tailor" your search. You'll find this necessary because the Internet contains *too much* information. (Google search technology claims to search a database of more than three *billion* Internet pages—all in a matter of seconds.) The use of quotation marks, mentioned above, is one search "precision tool" at Google. If I had searched for Sam Lord's Castle without using quotes, the search would have returned every Internet page Google found containing the words "Sam" and "Lord's" and "Castle" in any order. Most of those pages would have had nothing to do with the travel attraction on Barbados. The use of quotation marks to hold the three words together, in order, "narrowed" my results, in Internet jargon, to only those pages containing the exact term "Sam Lord's Castle."

Another technique for pinpointing pages that may be of use to you is the "minus" feature. You might want to *exclude* from your search certain types of pages related to your subject. For example, I might be interested in obtaining information about Barbados attractions *outside* the main port of Bridgetown, since I already have more than enough material concerning Bridgetown. One way to accomplish that would be to type the word "Barbados" in the search field, then type a space, followed by the minus character and the word "Bridgetown."

Tips for Internet Travel Research

On the Internet, you can find good airfares and other travel deals. But you have to search for them. Don't take the first deal you find, or one that turns up on the first page of hits your search returns. You also may find that your travel agent can find a better bargain.

Most travel destinations today have Web sites. You can obtain a wealth of information there, view and download photographs and even watch travel videos—free.

The Internet stores information on many of the other things we're discussing in this book. For example, at **medlineplus.gov** you will find information about various diseases, health conditions, medicines and treatment centers. After I've found information about a particular item at **medlineplus.gov**, I sometimes perform a Google search for additional information.

CAUTION: Remember that the Internet can "bite" you if you're not careful. There are a number of books on how to use the Internet safely.

On the other hand, you can use the plus character to narrow your search in a different way. If I'm looking for only historic sites on Barbados, rather than visitor attractions in general, I might type the words "Barbados" and "history" with a plus character (+) in between the two words. (That search phrase would NOT be enclosed in quotation marks, since that isn't the precise phrase I expect to turn up in the search.)

I have had great success finding almost every subject I've wanted to find using Google.

29

Identify Your Personal Things

I have some 2x4-inch shipping labels that can be fed through a computer printer. I'm going to label items which Rose and I plan to leave to our children. It's largely a matter of labeling things that came from my ancestors. I identify where they came from and their significance. I also plan to take pictures of these items and put them in a notebook with my comments about each item.

For example, my father worked in Alaska in the '20s, and he had a painting done by a painter who later became regionally famous, Sidney L. Laurence. My children know a little about that painting, but I'm going to leave them more details on the label and in the notebook. I've already communicated with the University of Alaska and a couple of museums there. In the event my children decide they don't really want the painting, I may choose to give it to one of the museums or to the university, and leave framed photographs of it to my children.

I have a vase and a pitcher that my Grandmother Wilkins gave me before she died—two of the very few things I have from this particular ancestor. She was born in 1871 and was in her 80s when she died, so these are extremely important to me. My children and grandchildren would never know that these came from my grandmother unless I identified them. So I'm going to label them on the bottom. The labels won't damage these items at all.

My Grandmother Pearce had a number of things that came to me through my mother and my aunt. She was an artist, and although I know of only three paintings she did, I want to indicate on the back that she painted them, because there's no signature on the paintings themselves.

We have the bed in which my aunt was born in the early 1900s. That bed had come to her from her mother, and had come to her mother from her grandmother. We think it came from Georgetown, SC—an important East Coast seaport in 19th-Century America—up the Pee Dee to the river town of Mars Bluff, and was delivered to where they lived in what was then Marion County (now Florence County). My daughter has the bed, and I want her to stick these details to the underside of the bed. When anyone in the future wonders where the bed came from, they'll have that information.

For you, other kinds of noteworthy items may be things you've acquired yourself. Rose and I have acquired a number of things that need to have labels attached because the children have no idea of their significance. We ran an art gallery 30 years ago, as sort of a pastime among other things we were doing. We presented shows for artists who eventually became relatively well known, and we bought paintings at those shows. I want to indicate on the back of them when we acquired them and perhaps some particulars about them and their creators.

Labeling is appropriate for furniture, paintings, china and large items. People forget to make notes about them. Then suddenly the ancestor's gone, and nobody knows anything about these items.

For china and silver, take pictures of the items and write notes about where they came from. An added benefit of this process is that you can make duplicate photos and data sheets for each of your children. You probably will want to photograph your labeled items as well. It's also a good idea for insurance purposes.

But take care that the descriptive material doesn't get hopelessly separated from the items you want to remember. The advantage of physically sticking a label to the back of an object is that the information is not nearly as likely to become lost.

If you have a photo collection, for goodness sake write the names of the people and the dates on the backs of the photographs. Happily for me—and as an exception to the rule—most of my ancestors identified many of the photographs that now are 75 to 100 years old. Twenty or 30 years ago, I sat down with some of those ancestors to look at and identify those photos which were unmarked. I wrote on the back the names of the people in the pictures. As a result, I know who most of the people are and approximately when the photographs were taken.

Unfortunately, I have other, older photographs—some of them at least 120 years old—on which no one ever wrote the basic information. I didn't discover these photographs until after my ancestors were dead. In most cases, I have no idea who these people were. In a few photos, I think I can make a reasonable guess who they were . . . but that leaves me just as frustrated, because I don't know for certain.

I've collected a large number of books over the years. Some were given to me by their authors, and some are worth at least a modest sum of money among collectors. The identifying information for books can be inserted loosely, if I decide I don't want to use an adhesive label. Either way, the descriptive data will let my descendants know the book is valuable, so they won't simply give it away after I'm gone.

I'm thinking seriously of giving to libraries some of the books in which my children may not be particularly interested. The same might be done with the things you collect, if you think your heirs might not want them. Libraries, public galleries, museums, universities, churches, schools, municipal government facilities and other entities may be ideal archives for certain items from your estate.

30

Give Some of Your Personal Items To Your Descendants Now

I did not live with my mother and father all my life. I lived with my aunt and uncle. They're all gone, and I now have all the items left by all of them. I simply don't need some of those things, so we've begun to give them to our children. Obviously, it depends on your age and your children's ages as to whether this chapter is appropriate for you.

Rose and I have accumulated a lot of things of our own over the almost 50 years of our marriage, and we no longer need some of them. We're beginning to pick out certain things to give to our children now. As our grandchildren grow older, we'll start giving some of those items directly to their generation. (In some instances, we give an object to one of our children with the understanding that it ultimately will go to a particular grandchild.)

Look at what you have. It's easy. Start at your front door and walk through your house, looking at every item. When you see something you really don't need anymore, let your children or grandchildren or other relatives have it to use.

One example: If you've inherited silver from both your mother and your spouse's mother, you now might have three sets of silver. Your grown children may have their own silver by this time, but even if they do, the sentimental value of their grandmother's silver is important to them. Consider handing it down now—perhaps for them to pass on to their children.

If the value of your proposed gift is greater than $11,000 in one year, discuss the gift tax implications with your tax advisor.

31

Give Up Some of Your Bad Habits

I don't smoke and I encourage people I know not to smoke. Many of them find it difficult to quit. It's probably the Number One reason we lose friends we don't want to lose. As you grow older, you find that one of the most painful experiences in life is losing a friend. If you smoke, try to quit. If you know people who smoke, try to help them quit.

If you are not sure what your bad habits are, ask your spouse or a close friend to list your five worst habits—and you reciprocate by making the same list for him or her. Now at least you have a list to work on.

32

Guard Your Health

You have to take charge of your own health. Nobody else is going to do it for you.

Have regular medical check-ups. It amazes me how many people tell about disturbing medical symptoms they're experiencing but will not go to the doctor. Even if you feel fine, when you enter middle age you should have at least an annual check-up. A doctor can catch fundamental warning signs that identify serious and potentially catastrophic conditions. If caught soon enough, many of them can be resolved. For older people, more vital tests need to be performed on the schedule recommended by a doctor.

If you have a family history of a particular ailment, you need to make sure your doctor knows about it. Routine medical examinations do not return warning signals for every known affliction. By periodically ordering an additional test or two for those specific concerns, your doctor may have a chance to help you avert hereditary problems before they become life-threatening.

Meanwhile, don't take your health for granted between routine check-ups—and don't count on your doctor as the sole guardian of your well-being. Read health reports and books that are written in terminology lay readers can understand. I've gone to the Mayo Clinic for many of my health problems, and I receive the clinic's regular newsletter (*Mayo Clinic Health Letter,* 200 First St. SW, Rochester, MN 55905; $27 a year). To me, the newsletter is tremendously helpful in keeping up with what goes on in the medical community. Another newsletter I find helpful is *Dr. Alexander Grant's Health Gazette* (P.O. Box 1786, Indianapolis, IN 46206; $24.95 a year). Each issue contains probably 10–12 excerpts from some of the leading medical journals and the medical press around the world. It provides good information about various health subjects.

Other health organizations and medical schools, including Johns Hopkins and Harvard, also put out good newsletters.

A huge volume of useful health information is on the Internet. An example is Medlineplus, a service of the National Library of Medicine and the National Institute of Health (**medlineplus.gov**). Whenever a doctor prescribes or suggests any new medication for me, I always go in, click on the name of the drug and print out the details about it.

Some diseases, of course, you have to manage yourself. Asthma, diabetes and acid reflux are examples. A doctor can prescribe the medications, but you have to perform your own treatment and regular tests. I have both asthma and acid reflux, and I've learned how to handle those conditions. My doctor can't manage them for me on a daily basis; I have to manage them myself.

You have to educate yourself on whatever medical condition you have. I have probably 25 books on asthma and acid reflux. I'm probably one of the few people who go to the library regularly and look in the *New England Journal of Medicine* index to see if there are any new reports of special interest.

I am a very strong believer in alternative medicine. I've read probably 25 books on vitamins and minerals over the last 20 years, and I've been taking vitamins about that long. Most of the vitamins and herbs I take have been determined to cause no side effects. I avoid those which have any possible negative side effects.

Several doctors in the past have told me people shouldn't take alternative products until they've been fully double-blind tested. My problem with that is that I'm 69-plus years old. I don't have time for researchers to double-blind test everything that might benefit my health. If current medical evidence indicates they won't hurt me, and substantial medical evidence indicates they're going to help me, I intend to take promising vitamins and supplements.

Interestingly, when I first started taking vitamins, the medical community generally was negative or, at best, indifferent toward them. But today, almost every issue of the two newsletters I mentioned above contains reports on tests that show some of the very positive things vitamins can accomplish. For instance, in *Eat, Drink and Be Healthy*, a book by Dr. Walter C. Willett of the Harvard Medical School, he recommends folic acid, vitamin B6 and B12 to protect yourself against heart disease. He has several pages explaining the benefits of various other vitamins and minerals.

Doctors likewise have begun to recommend certain remedies that alternative practitioners have been touting for many years. Since it's your life, you should read about things like this and decide for yourself what to try.

Of course, you have to take some of the things you read with a grain of salt. A report might represent a particular viewpoint based on a particular test which may have included 30 people or 30,000 people. In either case, it's helpful information because it keeps you aware of what's going on in the medical field. If there are issues you aren't sure of, you need to do additional research.

33

If You're Obese, Do Something About It

I read Dr. Robert C. Atkins' book, *Dr. Atkins' New Diet Revolution*, and went on the Atkins Diet about five years ago. In the first two months, I lost 15 pounds. I have kept all my weight off.

It's interesting that Atkins has been called a quack by some medical professionals in connection with a variety of subjects. One is his assertion that the low-fat pronouncements by dieticians and the government during the late 20th Century is why we have obesity today. One of Atkins' arguments is that in the process of making foods "low-fat," the food companies have added sugar and carbohydrates. The result is that people who eat those so-called "low-fat" foods are getting very fat.

A recent article in *The New York Times* by Gary Taubes reported on new studies that show some of the things Atkins has been saying may be correct. The author wrote: "If the members of the American medical establishment were to have a collective find-yourself-standing-naked-in-Times-Square-type nightmare, this might be it." *Diet Revolution* is a book you should read. It details what you should eat, provides recipes and tells you why you should change your diet. It recommends that you take a multivitamin, and it tells you what other vitamins you might want to consider.

You can obtain the article from *The New York Times*, or you can find it at Dr. Atkins' Web site (**www.atkinscenter.com**).

There is also a new book (see also Chapter 32) by Dr. Walter C. Willett, *Eat, Drink, and Be Healthy: The Harvard Medical School Guide to Healthy Eating*, that you should read. It tells you what's wrong with the Department of Agriculture's food pyramid. It also recommends a multivitamin and provides recipes for you.

Because different diets affect people in different ways, you must satisfy yourself or ask your doctor whether the diet you choose is one that is safe for you.

34

Take Time to Exercise

As you grow older, you find that regular exercise is necessary in order for you simply to keep doing the things you do.

I play a lot of tennis. Until a few years ago, I played softball regularly. I don't run, because I don't really like it, but I've raced sailboats, played volleyball and done a number of active things.

Recently I learned I have a moderate problem with high blood pressure. I realized I had not been exercising on a regular basis, other than playing sports. So I enrolled at our local wellness center, and I usually go there in the mornings. I try to walk on the treadmill three times a week (two miles at four miles per hour).

Sometimes I just walk in the neighborhood. They say walking is one of the most important forms of exercise.

Give some thought to doing whatever's necessary to maintain your good health through exercise so you'll be with us for awhile!

35

If a Loved One Is in the Hospital, Stay With Him/Her

Never let a loved one be confined in a hospital room alone. A hospital is a very dangerous place to be. I'm not talking about your illness; I'm talking about what happens inside hospitals.

I recently had to be hospitalized, and the doctor recommended that I take a certain dosage of medicine once a day. I took the prescribed dose in the morning, and in the afternoon, a nurse came in and tried to give me another dose. I told her I wasn't supposed to take it again that day. Later, when the doctor visited my room, I told him what had happened and he said he would get it fixed on my chart. Nevertheless, I was in the hospital two more days—and they tried to give me a double dose again, both days.

A problem can arise if your condition doesn't allow you to understand what medicines you're scheduled to take. You need a friend or relative present who knows what you're supposed to be taking and who can watch what they're doing. This is especially true if you're on an IV. A nurse may simply come and put in a new dose of something, without a word. These problems are most likely to occur on weekends and after shift changes.

A friend of mine recently had double knee replacements. He told me that while he was in the hospital, they gave him morphine via an IV. About two hours later, another nurse came into his room and gave him more morphine. He almost died. When he started having problems breathing, the patient next to him in the room called the nurses' station. If he'd been alone, he could have died.

That is not an unusual story. I've heard of similar hospital experiences from others. In fact, almost all the individuals with whom I've discussed this have given me their own families' example to substantiate my experiences and observations. I'm afraid the problem is going to get a lot worse before it gets better. I recently read an Associated Press story by Lindsey Tanner which stated that based on a study of 36 hospitals in Colorado and Georgia, "hospitals each make on average more than 40 potentially harmful drug errors daily." Keep in mind this is just one study.

I'm not in any way trying to discredit doctors, hospital workers or anyone else in the medical community. They all do wonderful work and save lives every minute of the day. I am just saying everybody is very busy. There's too much going on. Many hospital employees are overworked. I'm simply telling you that if you care about the person who's hospitalized, then stay with them. Know what medicines they're supposed to be getting, and make sure they don't receive too much or too little. You may save that person's life.

36

Thank Your Mentors Before It's Too Late

One of my great regrets is that a junior high school and later high school teacher—a major influence on my life—passed on before I had an opportunity to call or write to tell her how much I appreciated what she had done for me. A number of other people who impacted my life are still living. Contacting them is on my master list of things to do.

37

Study & Record Your Genealogy

This relates in part to our earlier chapter on the need to make audiotapes of your living ancestors, to get them to recall incidents from their early years and about their forebears.

In short, find out who your early ancestors were. For some people, it's very easy. For others, it's not so easy.

Most of my mother's family since the 1700s grew up within a 50-mile radius of where I grew up, so a lot of my genealogical information was easy to find close by. Tombstones alone contain lots of information. You'll probably find that other people, perhaps some of your distant relatives, already have conducted extensive research into your lineage. If you have any relatives who are members of a genealogical group like the Daughters of the American Revolution, this can help you quite a bit because they've been required to establish the fundamental information about their lines of descent. You may also find books that have been written about a particular ancestor. Some of your predecessors may be mentioned in history books about the region in which they lived.

Another primary source of information about genealogy is the Mormon (Latter Day Saints) Church's Family History Center in Salt Lake City. Visit its Web site, **www.familysearch.org**. It also has facilities around the country where citizens can go to search for ancestral data. It has amassed a tremendous amount of information.

You'll also find a wealth of information on the Internet. There are, for example, surname sites for the names that might match your relatives' names. You can post an inquiry online about who you're looking for. I conducted a search for one of my family names, "Pearce." I needed to know who Silas Pearce's father was; Silas lived in the late 1700s and early 1800s. I made contact with a woman on the Internet who also was searching for a Pearce relative. She suggested I might find help from a lady living in Clio, a small hamlet in South Carolina. I phoned the person in Clio, passed along greetings from my newfound Internet friend who knew her, and asked her, "Can you tell me who Silas Pearce's father was?"

She said, "Hold on a minute." Keep in mind she was not related to the Pearces. She went and got out some of her records, and when she came back to the telephone she told me, "Silas's father was Dixon, and Dixon's father was Thomas."

"How in the world do you have that information?"

She said, "Well, I've got copies of deeds and estate files from those eras. Let me give you the refer-

> ### *Friendly "Ghosts" On the Internet*
>
> Once you become active on the Internet, it just might happen that your *ancestors* will come looking for *you*!
>
> An author friend of mine used the Internet to spread the word about his new book to groups of mystery and history aficionados. Another author in the Southwest, reading one of his postings, noticed his last name was her maiden name. She happens to be keenly interested in genealogy. Curious, she visited his Web site and discovered from his biographical information that he lives in South Carolina—the colony from which her own forebears had migrated westward. She introduced herself via e-mail, asked one or two questions about his ancestry and quickly established that they had the same great-great-great-grandparents. She provided him with her own research details about their earlier lineage extending back two-and-a-half centuries, much of which he didn't know.

ences. You can call the state Department of Archives, and they'll provide you with your own copies."

I did, and sure enough, I found in the "whereas" clauses to those deeds a litany of information that told, among other things, who Silas Pearce's father and grandfather were.

It's fun. I was chasing one of my Wilkins ancestors who lived in Suffolk, VA, and I ultimately hired a very nice genealogist in Suffolk. She obtained probably a hundred pages of information for me about this particular ancestor. She couldn't take the lineage as far back as I wanted to, but I gathered quite a bit of knowledge about that ancestor and his father—and I haven't given up yet.

The archives department in your state will be able to help you. Several Internet sites also are fine places to begin your work: **ancestry.com**, **familytreemaker.com**, **genealogy.com** and **rootsweb.com**. I use a software program called Family Tree Maker (check with **genealogy.com**). I've entered all the information I've found about my ancestors into the program. It's a very effective piece of software that allows you to gather and organize your family tree. Also, a number of books on genealogy probably are available at your local library or bookstore. It will be helpful for you to read them before you get too deeply involved. There is a huge Web site, *Cyndi's List of Genealogy Links* (**www.CyndisList.com**), that you may want to explore.

Reestablish Family Ties

Consider organizing a family reunion for one branch of your family. Or if someone else has already done it, work on a present for them all. Get in touch with all these relatives (who are descended from this ancestor) and get the basic genealogical facts from them (name, date of birth, spouse's name and date of birth, date of marriage, names of children and their dates of birth and the same information for the children if they are married). Enter this information in Family Tree Maker and you will be able to print it all out in a booklet that each of them can keep and treasure. You can include addresses and phone numbers as well. Make sure the booklet includes as much of the same information about your ancestors as you are able to find. You can also print out a chart that will show everybody in that lineage. I enjoyed doing this for my Wilkins clan, and Rose did it for her Truesdale clan.

38

Plan What You're Going to Do When You Retire

I have many friends who never plan to retire. They love what they do, they want to do it for the rest of their lives, and in many cases that's basically all they do. They have few outside interests, and they're perfectly happy that way.

But a lot of other people *do* want to retire. The problem, for some of them, is that they, too, are married to their jobs at the moment and have few outside interests. I've read research that shows people who have not planned what they will do when they retire have a far earlier death rate than people who know what they want to do with the rest of their lives. Cultivating outside interests *before* you retire is important. Decide what your interests are, and plan how your retirement can allow you to take part in those activities.

If you think you don't want to retire, that's fine. But bear in mind that health at some stage may force you to retire. In that event, you need outside interests to keep you active and alert and doing something you like to do. So even if you don't *plan* to retire, you should start to develop outside interests for your later years, and start now.

39

If You Own a Business,
Determine Its Future

One of the biggest problems some of my estate planning clients had was that they were operating a business that in no way interested their children. They were trying to decide what to do: continue the business as long as they could, expand the business, sell it, etc. Many of these decisions depend on money and on their children's circumstances.

If you're in this situation, you need to plan. You need to decide what's going to happen to the business. After you die, can

---

Examine Your Business
As It Relates to Your Lifestyle

Are you trying to build an empire, or to enjoy life?

It is amazing, to me, how many people get caught up in their businesses. They're 65 years old, have a very good income and assets—and are still trying to buy new businesses rather than just enjoying the one they have, or life in general.

In my estate planning practice, I've had several clients who begged the basic questions: What are you doing with your life? Do you want to enjoy the rest of your life doing things you really like to do, or are you preoccupied with trying to build an empire? The reason in many cases is they just hadn't thought about it. They were simply doing what they always did.

The reality is that there are very few empire builders out there. Happily, two or three of my clients gave it serious thought and decided they really wanted to enjoy life. They sold their businesses to their employees or others, or turned them over to their children.

I know there are workaholics who aren't about to change, and I'm not going to try to change them. I would simply suggest that they try to find a way to inject more *fun* into what they're doing.

---

your spouse run it? Are there children, other relatives or employees who might like to run it or buy it? If not, the business is likely to drop in value fairly quickly after you're gone. Your heirs might not be able to get as much for it as you might get if you sell it during your lifetime. Obviously, your situation might not be at all like this. The purpose of this chapter is not to tell you what to do with your business. It is to tell you to "plan."

Without a plan, you have major problems. If you have children or other heirs who don't get along, those problems are going to be magnified.

40

Make an Estate Plan

There are very good lawyers in this field. You can find them in *Best Lawyers in America* or the American College of Trust and Estate Counsel directory, or through your state bar association. Be sure the lawyer you select to help you plan your estate—especially if it's going to be a taxable one—knows enough about the law to give you the optimal estate plan.

One of the most critical aspects of any estate plan is executing a durable power of attorney. This is a power of attorney that survives your incapacity. The advantage of it is that you designate a trusted loved one—usually your spouse or an adult child or children—to make critical decisions for you in the event you become incapacitated. These decisions will have to do with, for example, your health care and your property.

This does not give the designated person a right to spend your wealth and dispose of your property, except as you may direct, but it does allow them to manage your property and make health care decisions for you. In a durable power of attorney, you also can give your attorney (remember, this is not usually your lawyer, but is more likely your spouse or adult child or children) the authority to stop life support systems under certain circumstances. You obviously need a lawyer to advise you concerning the relevant laws of your state. You also need to discuss it with your spouse and children and tell them your thoughts.

The language is going to be legal language. But my own concept is fairly simple. I've told my wife and my children that as long as I have a brain and there's a chance I will survive, I want to be given a chance *to* survive. If the brain is gone and essentially I'm gone, then turn me loose. There are simple legal documents that let you determine this, but I recommend a durable power of attorney, which gives you a greater ability to describe what you want your attorney (agent) to do in specific health and property situations. You need a durable power of attorney for yourself and one for your spouse or your close friend.

Obviously, you also need complete estate plans for yourself and your spouse.

Encourage your adult children to have estate plans and durable powers of attorney—especially if they're involved in your business. Age really has nothing to do with this. Nobody knows when he or she is going to die. It could be tomorrow for a 25-year-old, or 40 years down the road for a 50-year-old. And you have to keep your estate plan up-to-date. Your lawyer or law firm should review your plan periodically, certainly no less frequently than every two or three years.

41

Consider Buying a Term Insurance Policy to Create an Estate

If you don't presently have an estate and you have a spouse and children who will need support, consider buying term insurance. For nonsmokers, term insurance is very reasonably priced. For example, a male nonsmoker, 35 years old, can buy a 20-year, $500,000 term insurance policy for between $300 and $650 a year. If you are a smoker or have been a smoker recently, the rate will be two to three times higher. (Does that send a message?)

You need to talk to your insurance agent and your lawyer to discuss your situation. In most cases, it can provide funds for family support and college in the event of your untimely death.

42

Stop Worrying

In almost 50 years of law practice, I've had a number of clients and friends who've worried about *everything*. It distracts them from their ability to enjoy life. It impacts their relationships with other people. It is almost an obsession, and it interferes with practically everything they do.

Years ago, I read Dale Carnegie's book *How to Win Friends and Influence People* and was very impressed by it. I later got a copy of one of his other books, *How to Stop Worrying and Start Living*. My copy of that book is dated 1944, but it seems to me everything in it is still applicable today, and it's still available at bookstores. At the end of the book are true stories of how different individuals conquered worry. I've recommended this book to every person I've known who's had a worry problem. *All of them* have told me it has helped.

Rather than try to reinvent the wheel and solve your worry problems within the confines of this small volume, I'm simply suggesting that you read Carnegie's book. The chapter titles alone lend a clue to the kind of insight you'll gain: "Don't Saw Sawdust," "Cooperate With the Inevitable," "The High Cost of Getting Even." Find the book, read it—and read it again when the worries come back.

Tune in the Positive

We certainly should be concerned about what goes on in the world around us—but not to the extent that our news media drive us into depression. Bear in mind that the "news mongers," as a colleague of mine calls them, sell newspapers and boost television ratings by grabbing our attention. The obvious way to grab people's attention is with loud, clanging, frightening alarms, not gentle whispers. When you unfold your daily paper or turn on a TV news show, do you expect to learn about all the *good* things that have happened? Hardly.

Perhaps we should demand more balanced good/bad news coverage. But since that's highly unlikely, learn to take the news with a grain of salt. Whenever it gets you down, go outside, listen to the birds and enjoy the flowers. Read a general interest magazine that tells you about a few of the countless *positive* things happening in your world. For every murder that occurs, there are hundreds of caring teachers, law enforcement officers, pastors, counselors and social workers who are striving diligently to put potential murderers on the right road. For every disaster that occurs, there are countless disasters averted. For every white-collar wrongdoing and alleged wrongdoing, there are untold, daily "rightdoings" in corporate America that continue to make our free enterprise system great. You rarely read or hear about the "rightdoings," but you must not forget that they far outweigh the wrongs.

43

Write a Book

The small volume you're holding is a book I've wanted to write for a long time. After casually compiling ideas as they came to me and pigeonholing them in obscure recesses of my mind over a period of years, I realized I needed to get them on paper and arrange them. Otherwise, some of my mentally pigeonholed items were going to be lost forever. So I decided at length to begin dictating my notes into a microcassette recorder. I did this over a period of months, often sitting on our gazebo overlooking a lake, sometimes while driving. I rambled a bit and committed a lot of repetition, but after it all had been transcribed into a word processing rough draft, I was able to see my long-dreamed-of book taking shape.

It was exciting. Obviously, much work remained to be done, but the bulk of the task—transferring my "raw" thoughts to paper (into the computer, actually)—was complete. What remained was to organize the chapters, fill in some blanks, move passages around, ferret out redundancies and merge some of the information, find better ways to express certain ideas, add relevant details that occurred to me upon reviewing the document, and improve some of the transitions. That work was comparatively easy and proceeded rather quickly, because the end of the project already was in sight and I was driven to complete it.

It's been said that everyone has at least "one good book" in them. (I hope you conclude this is something of a "good book" you're reading now, because I have others in mind, based on a fairly wide range of experiences.) But the point is that *you* undoubtedly have something to say, too. Simply recounting your experiences in the form of a memoir or "open diary" may be the most effective way to tell your story. You might feel you have the makings of the proverbial "great American novel" banging around in your brain. The only way to find out is to plot it and write it, and the only way to write it is to get started. If you enjoy writing poetry, compile some of your poems into a small volume, even if they're only to be published in limited quantity for relatives and close friends (like the family cookbook I discussed earlier).

I dictated my notes and sent them to my friend and associate editor of *Sandlapper, the Magazine of South Carolina*, Dan Harmon. He reduced all this to paper in a first draft that made some sense and then I worked on it with some refinements I wanted and sent it back to him for more comments. We then completed the final draft before I had some friends look at it to help me make sure I was on track. Without him, I would never have gotten this book out. (For a great collection of "history/mystery" short stories, read Dan's *The Chalk Town Train & Other Tales*; details are at his Web site, **www.danieleltonharmon.com**.)

If you feel inclined to write a book but don't know how to begin, hire Dan or some other professional to help you—perhaps a local newspaper writer or editor, or an English or literature teacher. You may find that you're capable of expressing yourself better than you give yourself credit for, and all you need is an experienced journalist to review your draft and offer suggestions. For me, since I'm not a very fast typist, the most practical process was to "write" my book verbally, during solitary quiet times, and turn over my dictation tapes to a journalist to transcribe and edit.

It's really no excuse to claim you're "not a writer" or you "never learned to type." If you have a story to tell and/or knowledge and experiences that you believe are worth sharing, find someone to help you transfer your book from the virtual realm of your imagination to the printed page.

44

Plan for Your Elderly Parent(s)

As with many things in life, the plan depends on money. There are a number of living arrangement choices to provide for your parent(s). They are: 1) stay at home without help (but with visits from nearby relatives), 2) live in an assisted living facility (you need to know what happens here, if the parent or parents can no longer take care of themselves), 3) live in a place that offers cottages or individual rooms and will provide nursing home care onsite when it is needed, 4) continue to live at home with several skilled sitters (either part-time or around the clock) or 5) live in a nursing home. Of course, they could move in with you or you could move in with them. For most people this probably would not be a good alternative, but it depends on *your* circumstances.

I think many people, if they can afford it, would like options 1 or 4. A number of our friends have selected 2 or 3. Very active people live in these facilities, and there are numerous things for them to do: play bridge or card games, socialize with their friends or engage in other group activities. These places usually provide three meals a day and many other services. They are not cheap, but many people select them because it makes the rest of their lives pleasant and they enjoy the other people who are there.

I guess the last choice for many but an absolute necessity for some (particularly Medicaid patients) is the fifth, a nursing home.

I am not an expert on this subject. My mother used Option 3. My aunt used 4. Rose's mother uses 1. (She is 94 and when she shows you how to touch your toes, she actually can touch her *palms* to the floor.)

The purpose of this chapter is to urge you to discuss this with your parents, explore the options and their costs in your area, and try to plan in advance.

45

Make Measuring Your Children & Grandchildren Fun

When our grandchildren come to our house, the first thing they do is go to the wall by the refrigerator and check to see if they have gotten taller. On this wall since about 1990 we have made each grandchild stand by the wall, put a little felt-tip pen mark at the top of his/her head and the date and first name of that grandchild. They delight in seeing how much they have grown, especially in comparison to the other grandchildren.

We also have all the adults do the same and the wall is a hodgepodge of names, dates and marks. Several years ago two Russian women basketball players stayed with us for a week while they were practicing for a game with the University of South Carolina's women's basketball team, in preparation for the Olympics. So "Zhanna" and "Elena" (both about 6 feet 2) are still on the wall. One of our dear friends who died recently was the tallest at 6 feet 6.

I almost forgot to include this chapter among the "50 things" until our oldest grandson, who just turned 15 and is 6 feet 1, reminded me. Thanks, Gregory!

46

Add More Humor to Your Life

I love to tell jokes. I like being in a group where we all tell jokes. The joke someone else tells reminds me of another. Some of the jokes are mild and some are more risque. It depends on the crowd.

I have some old tapes, both video and audio, of comedians of long ago going through their routines. I loved Red Skelton, Jack Benny, Bob Hope and others doing their thing. There were a number of old television programs that ran on and on with great comedians: Jackie Gleason, Fred Allen, Carol Burnett. Watch a comedy movie. Buy a Victor Borge or Carol Burnett or Red Skelton video collection, or a vintage Bill Cosby or Smothers Brothers CD set. When you go to the circus, pay special attention to the clowns.

Learn how to tell jokes and funny stories. They're fun to tell and fun to hear. The Internet is loaded with joke sites, from mild to less than mild. Find some new ones and have fun.

Laugh a lot. Find humor every day. You will be a happier person.

47

Learn How to Say No

I have friends who are incapable of saying "no" when some-one asks them to do something they don't want to do. By saying "yes," they are taking time away from things they would rather do.

Periodically, you are asked to do things you really don't want to do but, because of family or business reasons, you must say "yes." For the other things you want to say "no" to, learn some nice ways to say it: "I'm sorry but I'm going to be out of town that weekend" (and if you are *not* going to be out of town, then change your plans and be out of town, doing something you want to do). Or, "I'm sorry. I can't because X has asked me to help solve a certain problem." Or, "I have more on my plate than I can possibly do now." See if you can teach yourself to use this one: "I'm sorry. I just can't do it. I wish I could, but I can't."

You obviously are smart because you are reading this book ☺, so design you own method of saying "no."

48

Don't Let Problems Hang Over You

The list is the cure for almost all problems. Make a list of the problems that are hanging over your head and then systematically start dealing with them and checking them off the list. You will be amazed at how good you feel as the list gets shorter and shorter.

49

Prepare Now for When You're Gone

Before you die, you should decide whether you want to be buried or cremated, and where. You need to discuss that with your spouse, your adult children or whoever else might be involved in making those arrangements. It's a subject people don't care to talk about, but if you don't deal with it ahead of time, the folks you leave behind are placed in a position of having to deal with it during their highly stressful period of immediate grief. They have only a short time, usually under duress, to make funeral arrangements, church service arrangements and other decisions.

If you're going to be cremated, do you want your ashes in a cemetery or spread over an appropriate area? If you plan to be buried, buy a cemetery plot. Know where you want to be buried. Decide which funeral home you want to handle your funeral. If you want specific music or readings at your funeral, let your survivors know that. If you want a graveside service rather than a church service, and if that wish might differ from what your spouse wants, you need to duke it out with your spouse before you die. Obviously, the survivor will control the decisions, but in most cases they'll do the things on which you insist.

Consider writing your own obituary. At least, jot down things you want included in your obituary, or discuss them with your spouse, a relative or a close friend. (Remember, though, that if you don't leave details in writing and both of you go in the same accident, then you haven't accomplished your objective.)

When you give the funeral home the wording for an obituary, emphasize that the obituary is not to be edited.

50

Be Sure to Include Your Children & Grandchildren In Some of Your 50 Things

Rose and I had four children under 6 years of age. Some of the most wonderful days of our lives were doing things with them. They were involved in almost every aspect of our lives until they had all gone off to college. Much of this book is being written in the year that our youngest reaches 40, but I can't tell you how important it is for you to be involved in their lives—and my guess is that I don't have to tell you. You already know.

We are lucky. All of our children live within 10 minutes of our house. We have seven grandchildren. We usually celebrate each birthday at our house. There is at least one birthday party each month with everybody here.

Conclusion

I have had a lot of fun writing this book. If you get only one or two ideas from the book or if you change one thing in your life as a result of reading the book, I will have accomplished my mission. Make your list! Change your life for the better!

Postscript

"Short Term" Is the Only "Sure Term"

Plan your life as if you may have only a year or two remaining on earth. When I was younger, I never worried about that. I bought wine that I planned to drink five years later. I saved money to take trips in the future. Now I'm 69 years old, and I don't do that anymore. I buy wine to drink, not to store. I schedule trips for the near future, not for 2010.

If you can afford to do things and you've already provided substantial assets to your children, then do those things now. It's okay to spend your money on yourself. I tell people in general and my children that my estate plan is: *The last check is going to bounce.* Obviously, it won't, but this usually gets a laugh.

This life-planning strategy is especially important for people older than 50. Who knows how much longer you're going to be here? Do those things which make you and your spouse or your close friend happy, and do them straightaway.

By the same token, if you're committing time to something that does not make you happy, consider giving it up and getting on with your life, unless there's no alternative. Until recently, I'd been serving voluntarily on a board of directors. At an annual meeting, I had to listen to three-and-a-half hours of complaining which accomplished practically nothing. It dawned on me that life is too short to be spending large chunks of your time in futile, frustrating endeavors. I'm now, happily, an ex-member of the board.

Appendices

Obviously, much information is available on the Internet and in books about travel. What follows are observations based on some of my experiences.

Appendix I: Travel Destination Decisions

You need to decide where you really want to go. My favorite city in the world is Paris. We've spent 17 days there. In an Internet "chat" session, I gathered information from an expert in European travel. I obtained the name of a hotel in Paris that costs about $80 a night. It's a small hotel, but it's in an absolutely great location near the Luxembourg Gardens. It's within walking distance of most of the city's major attractions, and for other Paris destinations, it's within two blocks of a subway station that allows you to get there.

Our favorite place in Paris is the Musée d'Orsay, an old train station that's been rebuilt into a great art museum. We were not particularly overwhelmed with The Louvre. It was too big, too crowded for our taste. For some people, it's wonderful, but not for us.

I like London. We've been there several times. London has a wonderful advantage for many American travelers: They speak a similar language there! Australia and New Zealand are high on my list, but you need at least two weeks (preferably one month) for this trip.

The Greek islands are high on our list to visit. We haven't gotten to go yet, because every time we try to plan a trip there seems to be some new unrest in the Middle East or that part of the world.

I think we may schedule a trip to South America. Some of the *Yorktown Clipper* cruises (See Appendix IV) have offered extremely good rates to the Galapagos Islands and other offshore destinations.

In this country, there's no place better than New York City. It's crowded, it's an aggravation, it's expensive, but it's a place we like to go periodically.

I love art. When a major art exhibit is scheduled, I want to go see it. I went to see the works of Norman Rockwell in Atlanta; Vincent van Gogh in Washington, DC; Claude Monet in Chicago.

Probably one of my favorite cities in America is New Orleans. It has everything: food, unusual things to buy, nightlife. But my favorite activity in New Orleans is the Jazz Fest the last two weekends of April every year. They have eight different stages operating simultaneously, from about 10 a.m. till 5 p.m. They have had spectacular acts, from Little Richard to Jimmy Buffet. There are 50 or more stars each year, and the music is broader than just jazz. One fare lets you in, and you can spend the day. Restaurant booths carry crawfish étouffée and other New Orleans fare prepared by people who really know what they're doing. If you like jazz or similar music and you've never been, it's definitely worth attending.

They also have a wine festival there. Of course, Mardi Gras has made New Orleans famous, but I've skipped that. Too many people, not my thing—but it might be yours.

Boston is one of the nicest cities in the Northeast. At the other end of the continent are wonderful places like San Francisco, Napa Valley, San Diego, Seattle and Vancouver. Obviously there are many, many others.

And don't leave out Charleston, SC, and Savannah, GA, two of the nicest cities anywhere.

Reader's Digest has published several books that describe the 50 or 100 best places to visit in this country. Most of those trips are inexpensive. Your selection of a motel or hotel will depend on how much money you have. Rose and I have found that we can be very comfortable in mid-range motels that cost $50–100 a day. Most of our time is going to be spent doing things and visiting various attractions; the motel is just our place to sleep.

But again, you have to decide what *you* like and where *you* want to go, and make that list we've talked about. I have friends who enjoy biking trips and walking trips. Neither of those is for me, but if they interest you, all you have to do is log onto the Internet, and you can find more of those kinds of trips than you'll ever have time to take.

Different kinds of trips are sponsored by universities and by institutions like the Smithsonian and both national and regional museums. In some cases you have to be a member to participate, but the savings you can realize on tours of that nature might justify the cost of joining the museum society or the alumni association many times over. These trips generally are not only economical; they usually feature some outstanding guides to help you get the most out of your time. And in many cases you will be traveling with people you might know.

If you like to gamble, you probably know where those kinds of destinations are: Biloxi, Foxwoods, Las Vegas, Reno, Atlantic City and elsewhere.

Las Vegas, incidentally, now has a reputation as a fun destination even for tourists who *don't* gamble. You can book a hotel and enjoy excellent meals at extremely reasonable prices—or, if you want to splurge, you can find a place that'll take all your money. To me, probably the most spectacular feature in Las Vegas is in front of the Bellagio Hotel. There is a series of waterspouts—perhaps 1,000—that rise and fall in time with music. When the accompanying music is something on the order of the *1812 Overture* and it reaches its climax, several of the larger waterspouts in the center shoot water as high as maybe 300 feet. I've stood there for literally hours on end, just watching the show.

Of course, Las Vegas has a lot of other shows that are worth taking in, some of them free. Some of the casinos have entertainers in bars, and all you have to do is go in, sit down and listen to them.

One of the best ways to begin researching your places to go in the United States is to go to the library and look through the travel books. There's no need to *buy* dozens of travel books when you can borrow all you need from a public library.

In some circumstances, your career determines your travel destinations. During the 1970s and '80s, I was very active in the American Bar Association. Each year, the ABA has an annual meeting and a mid-year meeting. Additionally, I was active in two sections of the bar, and each section holds its own meetings in fall and spring. So Rose and I would attend as many as six to eight ABA-related meetings a year, held all over the country. I was also active in other professional groups that met all over the country. We've been to every major city in America. While we were there for the meeting, it naturally gave us an opportunity to see something of the city, enjoy the food and visit some of the attractions. This kind of travel, for me, was tax-deductible because I was making those trips in connection with my profession. Rose's expenses, of course, were not deductible, but the fact that my own share of the travel, lodging and dining costs could be written off was a significant incentive. If those kinds of trips are available in your profession and you enjoy travel, you certainly should make an effort to include them in your schedule.

Appendix II: Festivals

It's amazing: In South Carolina—a fairly small state—we have at least one festival every weekend, year-round. In "festival season" (April–September), you can probably choose from as many as 10 or 12 different festivals in different towns to attend any given weekend.

The range of festival subjects here is unbelievable. (Take a look at the calendar of events listed on the "What Goes On Here" page at *Sandlapper Magazine's* Web site, **www.sandlapper.org**.) Most events are thematic, and many relate to food. For example, we have an oyster festival, a watermelon festival, a peanut festival, a grits festival, barbecue cook-offs, several peach festivals, at least one Catfish Stomp, an Okra Strut and a Chitlin Strut. (Chitlins are deep-fried hog intestines.)

Other festivals in our state have cultural focuses. Camden has a Blues Festival; Hartsville has a Jazz Festival. Even small villages join the fun with their bluegrass, gospel and country music festivals. Columbia has the Three Rivers Festival, which has three main stages for music. Beach music and R&B are on tap at numerous festivals in this part of the country.

Meanwhile, we have arts festivals, flower festivals, ethnic festivals, international festivals and festivals that highlight everything from horses to sport fishing. A few of our best events are simply community celebrations that take their names from something related to a towns' history or regional renown. By far our most famous festival is Spoleto Festival USA, a 17-day *tour-de-force* in Charleston that showcases performers and attracts visitors from all over the world each May. Spoleto has grown so big that it has spawned a separate but related Piccolo Spoleto Festival, held at the same time.

Admission to most festivals is free. In some cases, the entertainment likewise is free. You pay for your food, of course, but for the most part, festival going costs little money and is a fun way to spend a day or a weekend. This provides an excellent, entertaining opportunity to learn more about your state or an adjoining state. In many situations, you can combine your festival excursion with other day trip or two-day trip destinations.

Find out about the festivals scheduled in your state and region. There are many you may not know about, some of which you really might enjoy.

Appendix III: Day Trips

Now that Rose and I have a little more free time in our lives, day trips are among the most fun things we do. We'll pick out a destination not far away that we've never seen, or a spot we like which we haven't visited in a long time. We sometimes plan a day trip series. We try to obtain local tourist information in advance to provide guidance on what to look for in that particular town or area: old churches or other historic sites, perhaps: canals; rivers or lakes; gardens—whatever that place is known for. Sometimes you can pick this up from a chamber of commerce or visitor's center. More and more regions and municipalities—even small villages—offer tourist information on Internet sites. Almost always, Rose and I take the back roads, avoiding the interstates. We've made countless day trips around South Carolina, and we've enjoyed every one of them.

You can learn a lot about the place you live and the places nearby. For people who work, most day trips have to be made on weekends, but for retired people or workers who have flextime, they can be scheduled during the week when destinations and travel routes are less crowded. You can drive to an area of interest, visit the shops, find a nice little place to eat, see whatever there is to see, meet some of the people who live and work there and get yourself back home by dark. Take photos, both at your destination and en route. For Rose and me, stopping to take pictures of old Post Offices has become one of our hobbies. At the town shops and sometimes at nondescript roadside barns with hand-painted ANTIQUES and COLLECTIBLES signs, we've made amazing finds. We've found marvelous old books. We've found unusual crafts at reasonable prices. We've found any number of small treasures that so many people miss simply because they won't spend the time to get out and discover these things.

When I first started practicing law, I had to travel to courts all over the state. I would ask friends in those places where to eat, and they usually told me, in so many words, to "stop where the parking lot's full." Believe me, that's invariably been an excellent rule to follow. Today, when Rose and I go to an unfamiliar town and see two or three restaurants, we tend to eat at the one where the parking lot's full.

Visit your state parks. These inexpensive half-day and day trips may turn out to be far more interesting than you expected.

Some one- and two-day trips are ideal for taking the children. On others, it might be appropriate to arrange for the youngsters to remain at home.

Rainmaking on a Sultry Day

At McClellanville, an especially interesting South Carolina coastal village, we were eating lunch on the screen porch of a restaurant that had been converted from an old store dating to the 1930s—very rustic. The building had a weathered tin roof, and it sounded like it was raining, but we didn't see any rain outside. We learned they had a device that sprayed water on the roof to keep it cool. The raindrop sound was an unintentional effect, but on a steamy southern summer day, it was a serendipity and indescribably pleasant experience.

McClellanville was one of our all-time favorite day trips. It's a charming locale with interesting shops. I bought a hand-carved model of the historic Morris Island lighthouse near Charleston Harbor. As meaningful to me as the carving is the memory of that excursion.

Appendix IV: Ships

Windjammers—(800) 327-2601, www.windjammer.com

I love sailing. My favorite kind of trip—Rose doesn't necessarily agree with me—is a sailing cruise. We've done 13 weeks over about 10 years on Windjammers in the Caribbean. We've seen almost every Caribbean island at least once, many of them several times. The Windjammer organization has five ships ranging in size from one that can accommodate 90 passengers to one that can accommodate 150. These vessels are 250–300 feet long with three or four masts. Wherever they go, they rely mainly on wind power. They use the engine in certain circumstances, but primarily they're sailing ships. If you don't like sailing, you should not go on these cruises.

The cabins are small, the accommodations rustic. In most quarters, the shower is in the bathroom so when you take your shower, the shower water runs on the commode. The food is very good, though they don't offer a lot of variety. Each morning they offer Bloody Marys, each evening Rum Swizzles and hors d'oeuvres before dinner. Cruises are reasonably priced, ranging from about $800 to about $1,300 per person (not counting airfare).

They go to almost every island in the Caribbean on one ship or another. You typically arrive at the departure port on Monday and return on Saturday. They offer a "stow-away night," which means for an extra charge you can arrive on Sunday and spend that night aboard ship. Some of my favorite islands include St. Bart's, Iles des Saintes, Anguilla, St. Martin, the British Virgin Islands and Grenada. People who normally sail on Windjammers are people who like to swim, snorkel, sail and enjoy the beach.

Windjammers certainly aren't for everybody. Some passengers get seasick, because if the wind is very strong, there is a fair amount of movement. For other travelers, Windjammer routines and dress codes are too laid-back. (I like the dress code for dinner: "Wear a clean T-shirt if you have one.") Guests aboard ship have a lot of flexibility.

Bare-Boat or Crewed Small Sailboats

Rose and I have taken one bare-boat (you-sail-it-yourself cruise) on a 38-foot catamaran with three other couples in the British Virgin Islands for one week. It was great. We also took a trip starting in St. Martin and going to a number of places including St. Barts on a 52-foot single hull sailboat with a captain and a cook. Surprisingly, the captain and the cook didn't cost that much. It was nice because you could steer all you wanted to, but when it came time to anchor and worry about the dinghy, that was the captain's problem. The cook handled all meals—and that alone helped make it a great trip for Rose. We chartered with the Moorings (**www.moorings.com**). This type trip is on our list to do again. Both of these trips are in our top 10.

Star Clippers—www.starclippers.com

We also like Star Clippers, which has larger, more elegant vessels. They also are true sailing ships, with four or five masts. These ships carry 150–220 passengers. We've sailed one in the Mediterranean and one in the Caribbean. On our Mediterranean cruise, there were probably fewer than 10-percent Americans onboard, but there were a large percentage of English-speaking passengers.

They like for you to wear a collared T-shirt to dinner. The dining room and the food are very elegant. This company offers trips in the Grecian isles and all over the world. These cruises are more expensive, and the trips are a little longer—normally seven days.

INTRAV Clipper Cruise Line—(800) 325-0010, www.clippercruise.com

We also have made a number of trips with the Clipper Cruise Line. These are not sailing ships. They have several ships. The *Yorktown Clipper* is a small, shallow-draft ship that carries about 140 passengers. It's more upscale than a Windjammer—you're expected to wear something a little tidier than a wrinkled T-shirt to dinner (maybe a collared shirt). They have wonderful chefs. What I really like is that they offer half-portions. That means if you see several things you really want to try, you can have a half portion of one and a half portion of something else.

The vessel has a nice, small lounge, and passengers can play bridge and do other things together. On Clipper routes, you can observe a rich variety of birds and plants and natural history. Most of these cruises provide at least one naturalist aboard. They carry Zodiac boats that take you to islands and inlets you normally would not be able to access. We've done the Copper Canyon trip—a train excursion connected to one of their cruises in the Sea of Cortez. We've also been to the Lower Caribbean on a Clipper.

One trip I haven't taken yet but hope to, if the world situation will ever straighten itself out, is a river cruise from Amsterdam down to Switzerland. It's inexpensive—about $1,100 per person for a week. The riverboats stop in a major European city every day. INTRAV handles some of these cruises.

Large Cruise Ships

I'm not a fan of large cruise ships, but a lot of people prefer them. On a big cruise liner you can dine at four or five restaurants with excellent food. You can enjoy good entertainment nightly and sometimes during the day. Most of them have gambling. They stop at nice ports of call.

The drawback, to me, is that they have too many people. But it is a very inexpensive way to enjoy yourself, if you like being around a lot of people. Cruise lines offer incredible deals, because a big cruise ship is hard to fill. As the departure date comes and they start to get nervous, they may make you an extremely good deal. You can go for a week sometimes for under a thousand dollars. We've done a few of those, and I enjoyed them, but I would rather take the small ships.

Although I generally don't enjoy large cruise vessels, one type of cruise does appeal to me. One of these days, Rose and I plan to book passage aboard a *theme* cruise ship. We like music; we like to dance. Theme cruise companies have offered several blues, jazz and rock-and-roll cruises.

For families traveling together, some cruise ships have special programs for children.

Win the "Keys" to Your Grandchildren's Hearts

Since we've had grandchildren, Rose and I have begun to bring little gifts back for them from our trips. But we've found that if you have too many grandchildren, this can create a problem. They may be very unhappy about who gets which gift. It also takes up formidable space in your return luggage.

We now simply get each of them a key chain with the name of the country or the city on it—all basically the same. To our surprise, they seem to like those gifts (at least the younger ones). They hook the chains on their book bags to take to school. They have key chains from all over the world. I wish we'd started doing that earlier.

It may be even more meaningful to bring them back coins from different countries you visit. Foreign coins are fascinating. Many of them have pictorial engravings. A few are in multisided shapes. See if your grandchildren can figure out the foreign words. Besides giving them a token of your travel adventure, you may encourage them to begin a delightful collecting hobby that will last a lifetime. It also teaches them a bit about the country and culture you visited.

Give

50 Things to Do With the Rest of Your Life

To Your Friends & Colleagues

TO ORDER:

Please specify number of books

1-4 books ($12.95 each): _____ book(s) x $12.95 = $_____

or

5 or more books ($10 each): _____ books x $10 = $_____

S.C. residents add 5% sales tax $_____

Shipping and handling
    (for 1 book, $2; each additional book, $1 each;
    for 5 books or more, $6 total) $_____

Total $_____

My check for $_____ is enclosed.

Name: _____

Address: _____

City/state/ZIP: _____

E-mail: _____

Please make checks payable to R.P.W. Publishing Corp.
Mail your order and check to:
    R.P.W. Publishing Corp.
    P.O. Box 729
    Lexington, SC 29071